T
BIRD
BOOK

THE BIRD BOOK

Written by Rob Hume

Illustrated by Peter Hayman

KYLE CATHIE LTD

This first 2008 edition published by
Kyle Cathie Limited
122 Arlington Road, London NW1 7HP
general.enquiries@kyle-cathie.com

A catalogue record of this book is available from the British Library.

ISBN 978-1-85626-805-9

Conceived, designed and produced by
Duncan Petersen Publishing Ltd, C7 Old Imperial Laundry, Warriner Gardens,
London SW11 4XW

Editor Jacqui Sayers
Design pinkstripedesign.com
Editorial Director Andrew Duncan
Additional artwork Richard Allen

Printed in Spain by E.G. Zure SA

CONTENTS

Wildfowl – swans, geese, ducks 12-65

Gamebirds – grouse, partridge, Pheasant 66-77

Divers, grebes, Manx Shearwater, Gannet, Cormorant 78-99

Bittern, Little Egret, Grey Heron, White Stork, Spoonbill 100-109

Predators including kites, eagles, harriers and falcons 110-145

Water Rail, Moorhen, Coot, Crane 146-153

Waders and other birds of wet places 154-201

Seabirds – skuas, gulls, terns, auks 202-229

Doves, pigeons, Cuckoo 230-241

Owls, Nightjar, swifts 242-259

Kingfisher, Bee-eater, Hoopoe, Wryneck, woodpeckers 260-277

Larks, martins, Swallow 278-291

Pipits, wagtails, Waxwing, Dipper, Wren, Dunnock, Robin, nightingales 292-313

Bluethroat, redstarts, chats, Wheatear 314-323

Thrushes, warblers 324-361

Goldcrest, Firecrest, flycatchers, tits 362-383

Nuthatch, Nutcracker, treecreepers, Golden Oriole, shrikes 384-395

Crows, Starling 396-413

Sparrows, finches, buntings 414-455

About this book

Even if you never step outside to look at a bird, this book will give you a lifetime's pleasure: it is not only a simple but hard-working field guide, but the ultimate armchair birdwatcher's book. If you've never thought about birds before, just flicking through the pages and reading the short texts will enchant you.

If you already know something about birds and want to improve your birdwatching skills, then *The Bird Book* is also for you. It's not just a collection of pretty pictures: exceptionally detailed paintings work with expert text to enable you to separate every species. It simplifies identification, only mentioning complicating factors, such as male and female plumage variation, when they could be confusing.

Birdwatching can be tricky: some species look very similar, and sometimes unusual lighting can make a bird look unlike its normal self. In these situations, *The Bird Book* will enable you narrow identification down to one or two possibilities. For most encounters with birds, in your garden, in parks or on country walks, this guide is all you need.

The paintings

These are detailed and precise, with more than enough plumage and anatomical detail to separate each species. The artist, Peter Hayman, is especially respected for the accuracy of his anatomical proportions and his ability to paint every feather. He was an architect before becoming a wildlife artist, and perhaps because of this has an unusual respect for the underlying structure of each bird.

Artwork labels

If there is no label, there are no confusing variations in that species.

The text

Rob Hume's descriptions are an easy read for everyone, with little jargon and few technical terms – if used, they are explained. Above all, Rob Hume has described what the bird *is*, how it makes its living, as well as pinpointing its identification by discussing defining characteristics. Bird calls are notoriously difficult to convey phonetically, but Rob does so in the text. In isolation, it may be hard to make sense of them, but if you hear the bird, referring to the phonetic description could well confirm the identification.

The maps

Supported by a few simple words of explanation, these are always worth reading because birds are seen in different places at different times of year.

- Purple shading means the bird is resident – stays all year long.
- Red shading shows where a bird is a summer visitor, arriving in spring.
- Blue shading means a winter visitor – visiting the mapped area between autumn and spring, or passing through on migration.

Other features

A simple impression of size – always an important clue – shown by perching silhouettes.

Measurements in centimetres and weight – a back-up to the silhouettes, these give the bird's measurements from end of beak to tip of tail, and its bulk.

Flight silhouette – on a sky-blue background, this is enormously valuable for focussing on the overall shape and character of the bird. Sharpen your identification skill by covering everything except the silhouette, and trying to identify the bird from that alone.

Order of species – the birds follow broadly in a taxonomic (scientific) order, but simplified to group similar-looking species in consecutive pages.

Birdwatching basics

Some budding birdwatchers never recover from the frustrating discovery that out of doors, birds tend not to appear as they do in books. Small birds in a tree top look like dark dots against the sky. Waders on a pool rarely stay put while you note the colour of their legs and bills. The advice on these pages will help you to get over these hurdles.

Equipment

Binoculars are essential, except for some birdwatching in parks and gardens. Get the best you can afford, with a magnification between seven and ten. Go for 7x50, 8x40, 10x40 or 10x50. Take trouble to get the eyepiece adjustment exactly right for you. A telescope, best used on a tripod, gives much higher magnification than binoculars, but a narrower field of view, so is useful on an estuary, but not in a wood.

Clothing

Wear whatever is comfortable. White or bright colours can alert bird to your presence, but keeping quiet and still are more important. Plenty of pockets for notebook, bird guide, map and sandwiches are useful.

Keeping quiet

Birds have excellent hearing and, if they hear you coming, can move away long before you have seen them. Even in hides at reserves, keeping quiet is essential. Loadly hissed whispers can carry a long way. If you must talk, low subdued tones are best.

Keeping still

Birds are ultra-aware of movement. You can often get closer to a bird if you go straight up to it than if you move to one side: there is less apparent movement. But there's no substitute for keeping still. Sometimes, though, you can cruise past a bird in a car, then find it flies off if you stop. Sudden change seems to disturb most birds.

Even at long range, some birds – typically wildfowl – can react swiftly to the sudden appearance of humans. Keep down, keep out of sight, and stay still.

In a hide, don't put your arm out to point out the location of a bird. Describe where the bird is using a clock system eg "Four o'clock from the top of the tall pine".

Use the light

Best get the sun behind you: back-lit birds present as silhouettes – with little detail – while you are well lit. Conversely, use an expanse of sky to pinpoint a bird silhouetted in a hedge; then move around for a better-lit view.

Listen for calls

Most birds in woods or bushy areas are heard before they are seen. If you don't know what the calls are, at least follow them up. Calls are valuable in other ways, too. The sudden sharp 'tik tik' of a Starling alerts other Starlings – and you – to the approach of a sparrowhawk. The loud, excited chattering of swallows and martins announces the appearance of a Hobby. Often, a roosting owl is discovered by small birds, which then make a racket around it – known as mobbing.

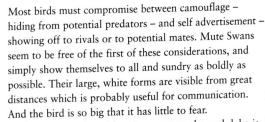

Mute Swan

Cygnus olor

Most birds must compromise between camouflage – hiding from potential predators – and self advertisement – showing off to rivals or to potential mates. Mute Swans seem to be free of the first of these considerations, and simply show themselves to all and sundry as boldly as possible. Their large, white forms are visible from great distances which is probably useful for communication. And the bird is so big that it has little to fear.

The common, bread-begging swan on the park lake is the Mute Swan. The Whooper and Bewick's Swans are wild, unapproachable and much more restricted in their distribution. See page 14. Mutes carry their heads tilted down, and their tails pointing up. The orange and black bill of an adult, with its black basal knob, is unique. Their grace, elegance of form and impressive beauty, especially in aggressive displays with wings arched above their backs and heads drawn back, are clichés, but none the less real for that.

Mutes are not entirely mute, making a variety of hissing and strangled bugling notes, none so musical as the other swans' calls. They have a unique characteristic, in that their wings make a loud, throbbing, rhythmic *whoop-whoop-whoop* in flight, quite distinct from the usual rasp and whistle of large feathers rushing through the air, which is heard from other large birds.

Mute Swan

Sparrow

Widespread, except in upland regions.

Adult

Juvenile

50cm. 8-14 kg.
Also see Whooper and Bewick's Swans, page 14.

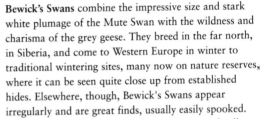

Bewick's & Whooper Swans

Cygnus columbianus

Bewick's Swans combine the impressive size and stark white plumage of the Mute Swan with the wildness and charisma of the grey geese. They breed in the far north, in Siberia, and come to Western Europe in winter to traditional wintering sites, many now on nature reserves, where it can be seen quite close up from established hides. Elsewhere, though, Bewick's Swans appear irregularly and are great finds, usually easily spooked.

They fly with slightly rasping wing beats, and call loudly, making a rounded, musical, sometimes even bubbling sound. On a misty day, when flocks are hidden somewhere across the wet fields or marshes, their calls echo around in a wonderfully evocative way.

The **Whooper Swan**, one of Europe's largest (equal in length to a Mute Swan), flies from Iceland to Britain between October and late March. They have increased dramatically on the East Anglian Ouse Washes, but are otherwise more likely in Scotland, the far north-east of England and a few odd places in Wales. They like undisturbed grassy places close to water – river valleys, coastal pastures and the like – and the lochans of western Scotland and the Hebrides. Whooper Swans have a wonderful loud, clanging chorus of bugling and trumpeting notes: groups often interact with raised wings and heads thrust forward, bills open wide as they call loudly.

Bewick's Swan

Sparrow

Winter visitor.

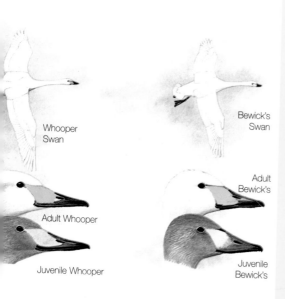

Whooper
Swan

Bewick's
Swan

Adult
Bewick's

Adult Whooper

Juvenile Whooper

Juvenile
Bewick's

Whooper Swan

Sparrow

Winter visitor to NW.

Bewick's Swan: 120 cm. 5-7 kg.
Whooper Swan: 145-160 cm. 8-10 kg.
Also see Mute Swan, page 12.

Bean Goose

Anser fabalis

Bean Goose

Sparrow

November to
February.

Of the large, 'grey' geese, this is one of the scarcest: in the Low Countries it is widespread in winter, with flock of hundreds, but in Britain is restricted to two or three regular sites and is otherwise a rare vagrant – an excitin find. Bean Geese breed in Scandinavia and Russia and move south and west in winter, liking old grassy pasture and ploughed fields, where they grub about for roots.

Wild geese have more elegant forms and more agile movements than their farmyard derivatives, but their obvious 'goosiness' makes them easy to identify as a group. Telling a Bean Goose from a Pink-footed, or a young White-fronted, however, is not always easy. In fact, a Bean is very like the commoner Pink-footed Goose, but less grey above, with a longer, less rounded head in profile, and a slightly longer neck. It has yellowish to orange legs, rather than pink. Confusingly, there are two forms: one with a shorter neck and smalle bill that is dark with a narrow pale band (much like the Pink-footed but with an orange band instead of pink), the other, a rangier-looking bird, with a bigger beak, more extensively orange. Both occasionally turn up in flocks of other geese, and it is an enjoyable challenge staring at them for hours with a telescope, trying to spo the unusual visitors.

1-89 cm. 3-4 kg.
so see Pink-footed Goose, page 18.

Pink-footed Goose

Anser brachyrhynchus

Pink-footed Goose

Sparrow

Winter visitor.

If it is the romance of the wild geese that you want, birds that fly in long skeins and V-shapes against coppery evening skies and glorious sunsets, or graze elegantly on remote marshes, then the Pink-footed Goose is your bird. Of the 'grey geese' – those that are predominantly grey-brown – this is the prettiest, with a round, dark head on a short but shapely neck, a small, dark beak crossed by a band of pink, and pale to deep pink legs. The dark neck makes a pleasing contrast with a pale fawn-buff breast and the almost blue-grey back, barred with narrow white feather edges.

A chorus of Pink-feet in flight is likewise a magical sound, full of urgency and nervous energy, a fast, deep, honking gabble interspersed with characteristically high-pitched *wink-wink* calls. In favoured places, such as the polders of the Netherlands, the coastal marshes of East Anglia in England and some Scottish estuaries, tens of thousands of them can be seen together, one of the finest wildlife spectacles that Europe can offer. The Pink-footed Geese that visit the U.K. breed in Iceland; those that spend the winter in the Low Countries breed in northern Europe and Siberia. In March, they each go their own ways, heading north again, making patterns against the sky and calling to everyone who listens, that spring is returning once again.

4-76 cm. 2-3 kg.
so see Bean Goose, Greylag Goose, pages 16 and 22.

White-fronted Goose

Anser albifrons

While the Pink-footed Goose may claim to be the most elegant of the 'grey' geese, the White-fronted is perhaps the most colourful, with its white forehead blaze, black belly bars and bright orange legs. Those that breed in Greenland visit western Scotland and Ireland in winter and have orange bills and darker plumage overall. The larger population from Russia, visiting the Low Countries and Eastern Europe in winter, look paler and pink-billed. The bill and leg colour help identify young birds that lack the black bars and white forehead – they are best told by the company they keep.

In Britain, the Russian White-fronts have declined and even disappeared from traditional haunts, as numbers have built up in the Netherlands – in mild winters, these birds simply don't need to move farther west. They gather in big flocks, of thousands, even tens of thousands in some places, feeding on low-lying, wide-open, wet grassy fields and marshes. Each evening, they move off to some safe roost on a lake or reservoir, flying in long lines and chevrons, typical of the romantic image of wild geese. They create a loud, ringing chorus, with sharp calls that seem to have a 'catch' in them, like *lyo-lyok* or *kl-yok*, creating a less even, less deep effect than a flock of Pink-feet, and not so harsh and clangorous as Greylags.

White-fronted Goose

Sparrow

Winter visitor.

Adult

Juvenile

cm. 2-3 kg.
so see Pink-footed Goose, page 18.

Greylag Goose

Anser anser

Greylag Goose

Sparrow

Wild birds, far north.
Introduced birds
widespread in UK.

In much of Europe, the Greylag is the common, year-round goose of marshes and wet pastures, breeding much farther south than most of the so-called 'grey' geese. In southern parts of the UK, it has been reintroduced, with mixed results: flocks of Greylags thrive, but have lost much of the romance of wild geese, neither migrating far nor being wary and unapproachable, as geese ought to be, and often in the company of the entirely alien Canada Geese. Nevertheless, tens of thousands of truly wild Greylags move south from Iceland and northern Europe in winter, often mixing with Pink-footed and White-fronted Geese.

Greylags, compared with these other species, are big and heavy, with more than a hint of the farmyard gander about them: they are, in fact, the ancestors of domestic geese. In flight, they show large areas of very pale blue-grey on the wings, above and below, and on the ground their heavy orange bills are distinctive. Their clanging, clattering, honking calls lack the music of Pink-feet (pages 18) and White-fronts (page 20): but it is wrong to think of them simply as inferior to these supposedly more refined species. Wild Greylags are, in themselves, impressive and evocative birds and, where they are winter visitors, mark the passing seasons as surely as swallows announce the coming of summer.

84 cm. 3-4 kg.
see White-fronted and Pink-footed Geese. pages 20 and 18.

Canada Goose

Branta canadensis

As the name suggests, this is a New World bird, brought
to Britain as an ornamental addition to large estates and
parks with sheltered, shallow lakes. It has multiplied and
spread to adjacent areas of mainland Europe, and has, in
many areas, become a controversial bird, apt to be
aggressive and messy. Many people like them and feed
them, so they have become tame, too, although larger
flocks still live on bigger lakes and reservoirs and feed
out on marshland and fields.

This aside, Canada Geese are big, impressive birds. A
flock in a distant river valley pasture on a misty
morning, or flying in to feed on a big field, can look
marvellous. They call loudly and often, with a deep,
repetitive honk or hoot. They are easy to see and easy to
identify: even juveniles look like dull adults, with the
characteristic barred brown body, big white stern, pale
breast and black 'stocking' on the head and neck,
marked by a broad white chin strap. Sometimes other
geese join them, especially semi-wild Greylag Geese and
a mixture of others gone wild from collections, such as
Barnacle Geese. Greylags (see page 22) and Canadas
have a tendency to hybridise occasionally, producing big
confusing, frankly ugly cross-breeds, with brown and
white heads and dark, yellowish or pink bills.

Canada Goose

Sparrow

All year. Mostly in S
and E of UK.

cm. 3-4 kg.
see Barnacle Goose, page 26.

Barnacle Goose

Branta leucopsis

The Barnacle is a so-called 'black' goose from the Arcti
It uses several isolated, restricted breeding areas on sub
Arctic islands such as Svalbard and in parts of
Greenland, and birds from each have small, traditional
wintering ranges in North-western Europe. There is ver
little mixing but all look alike. Look for them in The
Netherlands, Scotland's Solway Firth and on the Inner
Hebrides, especially the island of Islay, where many
thousands can be found between October and late Apr
In recent years, some semi-wild flocks have built up,
originally established from 'escapes' from collections.

Barnacles are truly immaculate birds, black, grey and
white, with a large creamy face set in a black head, neck
and chest (whereas the bigger Canada Goose is browner
has a narrower white chin strap and a pale breast). They
prefer coastal grassland and close-cropped, green salt
marshes, snipping off short shoots and leaves with their
small, rounded beaks. In the early winter many are
restricted to nature reserves, roosting on adjacent
estuaries, but they spread once the shooting season is ov

Barnacles don't produce the musical calls made by
grey geese. They yap like small dogs, making a loud,
formless but distinctive chorus. They also fly in more
ragged packs, sometimes more or less aligned, but not
often in the neat Vs and chevrons of the grey geese.

Barnacle Goose

Sparrow

October to April.

9 cm. 3 kg.
see Canada Goose, page 24.

Brent Goose

Branta bernicla

Brent Geese are small, neat, appealing geese of the sea
shore and adjacent farmland, easily distinguished from
the larger Canada and more boldy patterned Barnacle.
They do, however, come in two distinct forms in West
Europe. Those that breed in Siberia are very dark –
'dark-bellied' – and mainly spend the winter around th
North Sea, with some going to the south-west of Engl
and Wales. Those from Arctic Canada are paler benea
– 'pale-bellied' – and spend the winter in Ireland and i
north-eastern England.

On both forms, the whole head, neck and breast are
smoky black, except for a variable patch of white each
side of the top of the neck (missing on juveniles). They
are dull, dark grey-brown above. Juveniles are easily t
by narrow whitish bars across the wings: this is helpfu
to scientists who work out their annual breeding succe
which affects winter population numbers and varies
dramatically from season to season.

Brent Geese like mudflats and muddy creeks in
marshes, but many also feed on pastures and fields of
winter wheat. In places they have become remarkably
tame, but even then retain something of the charisma
'wild geese'. A flock flying over an estuary, filling the
with rolling, croaking calls (from which they get their
name), on a mid winter afternoon looks wonderful.

Brent Goose

Sparrow

October to April.

69 cm. 3kg.

see Barnacle Goose, page 26.

Shelduck

Tadorna tadorna

Geese are grey, brown, black and white in cryptic combinations; ducks are generally characterized by the females' streaky brown plumage (at certain times) and the males' dull, inconspicuous summer garb. Why, then should the Shelduck break the rules and be so striking bird at all times? Both sexes are boldly black and white with a rufous band around the front part of the body. The bill – with a big basal knob on the male – is the most vivid, vibrant red in the whole bird world. The juvenile is a drab, dull white, with brown-black marks and a whitish face.

The black and white is remarkably effective at hiding the bird against the gleam and contrast of a wet sandy beach or estuary, but in most circumstances the Sheldu stands out a mile. It is, perhaps, large enough to suffer from few predators in its beach habitat.

Most prefer wide sandy bays and estuaries, and nest nearby dunes, or in rabbit holes under bramble patche but a few pairs breed, instead, near gravel pits far inla In late summer, the young birds of the year are bunche together with a few proxy parents and the rest of the adults fly off to the coasts of Germany, where they mo in the safety of the vast mudflats of the Heligoland Big They then seem strangely scarce in most other areas, b soon return to be among the most obvious coastal bir once more.

Shelduck

Sparrow

All year, most British and W European shores.

cm. 950-1,400 g.
see Shoveler, page 44.

Wigeon
Anas penelope

Most ducks are exquisite creatures, but Wigeon are re
beautiful. They feed in dense flocks, all facing the sam
way, progressing steadily across a tightly-grazed marsh
wet field on their short legs, cropping the grass like tin
geese. The effect is striking, with so many replicated
shapes and patterns to delight the eye.

Males have white wing patches: even in summer or
autumn, when they are in 'eclipse' plumage and lack t
winter colours, they retain the white. In eclipse, they a
still a richer colour than females, looking quite red or
chestnut, with bright white bellies. Females also have
white bellies (unlike Mallards), and short dark legs, bu
are mostly browner or greyer. Their short, grey bills a
steep foreheads help identify them.

Wigeon

By late autumn and through the winter, males are
blue-grey, with pink fronts, black and white sterns and
brown heads, marked by a band of pale primrose on t
forehead. Teals look darker, without this yellow band,
and are much smaller, and more agile.

Sparrow

Male Wigeon also have a highly characteristic call: a
loud, challenging whistle, *whee-ooo*. Females don't
quack, but make a deep, rough growl. The mixture of
sounds blends nicely when a large flock takes flight. I
flight, Wigeon show long, pointed, swept-back wings
narrow, pointed tails.

Mainly autumn to
spring, widespread.

Female

Male

cm. 550-1,000 g.
see Teal, page 36.

Gadwall

Anas strepera

Gadwalls are curiously scarce, localized ducks, in many areas established from past introductions. They gather o reedy lakes in winter and disperse to breed around lowland rivers and pools.

They are large, but not so heavy-bodied as Mallards, and have a different profile, with a more slender, paralle sided bill and a steeper forehead. Their legs are more yellow-orange. Females show a sharply-defined, clear white belly, while Mallards are dark underneath.

Males are grey and pale grey-brown with a black rear end, while females are like female Mallards, streaky-brown, but rather more yellowish, with a dark-spotted effect. Both sexes have a square of white near the base o each wing, often showing as a narrow triangle on a swimming bird, or altogether hidden, but striking in flig

Gadwalls are rarely seen in large numbers together, although often mixed with many Mallards and other ducks. In such situations, especially in a flock of similar-looking, dull brown moulting birds in autumn, trying to pick them out at a distance on a reservoir or lake is goo fun and helps to sharpen your birdwatching skills.

Gadwalls are surface-feeders, dabbling at the edges of pools or filtering water through their bills to extract minute items of food. They often swim around Coots, waiting for the diving birds to bring up clumps of weed, and snatching whatever they can.

Gadwall

Sparrow

Localized but widespread. All year.

male

Male

Male

54 cm. 600-1,300 g.
see Mallard, page 38.

Teal

Sparrow

All year, but most
seen August to April.

Teal
Anas crecca

Of all the ducks, this is the smallest, most agile and most
like a wader in flight. Groups of teal sweep up if alarmed
and dash away, twisting as they rise almost like a flock of
Redshanks. They are widespread but local, needing shallow
pools, muddy reservoir edges, wet grassland and marshes,
fresh or salt: they are not everyday ducks found in
suburban areas. In summer, most breed in the north, or
high on bleak moorlands with rushy pools and streamside.

Drakes – as male ducks are called – look dark,
revealing their bright colours only at close range in
bright light. The sun picks out the deep green band on
the side of the dark brown head, and the creamy-yellow
triangle each side of the tail. From behind, the wings
may have a lilac or purple sheen from certain angles.
Females are mottled dark brown, with a light streak near
the tail. Both sexes have short, slim, dark grey beaks,
short grey legs and a patch of bright grass-green on the
wing, edged with buff and white.

A typical winter sound from a wet marsh is the ringing
call of the Teal: not nearly so loud and dominant as a
Wigeon's whistle, but a repeated double note, like *crik-
crik*. Females make a quick, low *quack*, but are generally
quiet birds.

Female

Male

cm. 200-430 g.
see Wigeon, page 32.

Mallard

Anas platyrhynchos

This is the common wild duck – but you could also call
a tame duck, as it is found in almost any habitat with a
little water, from a roadside ditch, a town pond or a pa
lake to large reservoirs, estuaries and coastal marshes.
pair or two may come for bread on a town-centre river,
or hundreds might fly in at night to feed in a cornfield.

In summer, males look like dark, reddish females, b
in the autumn they gradually develop their finest colou
which last through to the following spring. The head i
beautiful deep green, glossed with blue and purple, abo
a narrow white collar. Most of the body is grey, but th
rear end is boldly marked with black and white. The
central tail feathers curl upwards in a characteristically
flamboyant touch. Females are brown, streaked with b
and black, with whiter tails. Both have bright orange
and the rear wing has a patch of purple-blue, edged w
white each side. This shows well in flight as a dark ba
with two parallel white lines. There are many semi-
domestic variants in urban areas, especially, from all-
white to almost black.

Male Mallards are renowned for chasing females in
spring, part of their pairing and territorial behaviour.
They display with bubbling, whistling calls, while the
females make the classic loud, almost coarse, *quack*.

Mallard

Sparrow

Widespread all year.

Female

Male

cm. 800-1,500g.
o see Wigeon, Gadwall, pages 32 and 34.

Pintail

Sparrow

Mostly winter.

Pintail

Anas acuta

This is a superbly elegant bird. It is quite heavy-bodied, but has a long, slender, tapered neck and small, neat head, with a slim bill. The tail is also tapered and pointed, with extra long central feathers on the male. O the ground, it is short-legged. In flight, it looks like a b duck, with narrow, pointed wings.

Winter males have striking white foreparts, visible at great range, and a line of white stretches up each side c the neck. Females are similar to female Mallards, but a little paler, and greyer or more buff-coloured on plainer looking heads. They have dark bills and legs, without any orange. In flight, the female shows a long, thin line of white along the trailing edge of the wing, a valuable identification feature once learned. They are quiet birds but females may sometimes make a quick, subdued, staccato quacking.

Pintails spend the winter in flocks, mostly in small, well-defined areas on flooded grasslands, coastal marsh and estuaries. They are by no means universal or so easily seen as Mallards and are therefore always a pleasing event. One or two tend to turn up on reservoir among commoner ducks in autumn or winter, and finding them in this case can be a challenge.

Male

Female

-59 cm. 600-1,100 g.

o see Mallard, page 38.

Garganey

Sparrow

March to September,
generally scarce.

Garganey
Anas querquedula

This is one of the smaller ducks, a little bulkier than the
Teal. It is an oddity in Europe, being a summer visitor
from Africa, often arriving in March. In many areas, it
most familiar as an autumn migrant, when small family
groups are on the move and appear in mixed flocks of
moulting birds. At this time they are dull and brown an
something of a test, even for the committed duck-watch

Spring males are easy, with their dark heads decorat
with a bold white crescentic stripe and combination of
pinkish-brown and light blue-grey on the body. Autum
birds and females are more like female Teals, but have
subtly different face pattern, including a stronger stripe
over the eye, a dark band across the pale cheek and a
whiter spot near the bill. In flight, males have pale blue
grey forewings, females a greyish bloom, with two
narrow white bars on the hind wing (by contrast, the
Teal shows a weaker one at the back and a thicker one
the middle).

Garganeys breed on grassy marshes and wet meadow
with pools. These habitats have declined with the tren
towards a neater, drier, more productive countryside. In
autumn, you might see one or two on a shallow, lowla
reservoir, but the Garganey is not by any means a
common or familiar bird anywhere.

Female

Male

-41 cm. 350-400 g.
o see Teal, page 36.

Shoveler
Anas clypeata

The Shoveler's long, broad, heavy bill looks disproportionate at close range, but, in a distant view, seems to shrink into a less obvious, more normal duck beak. For this reason, telling a lone female Shoveler from a female Mallard can take a little time. When you get a close view, the bill is indeed a large shovel, usually pushed through shallow, muddy water as the duck swims forwards, shoulders almost awash, filtering out anything edible from the soup. Occasionally, Shovelers form a tight feeding flock, even spinning around slowly together. When they up end, just as Mallards so often do, their long, pointed wing tips are striking.

Because of their specialized feeding equipment, Shovelers are restricted to shallow fresh water and peaceful estuarine marshes, but are also often seen on reservoirs and flooded gravel pits. They are usually much less numerous than Mallards or Wigeons.

The male is obvious in his winter best, with a bright white front and black head, but in summer looks rufous overall, with a mottled whitish crescent on the face. The female is streaky brown and orange-legged, like a Mallard, but has pale blue forewings that are obvious in flight. Shovelers' wings make a loud *whoofing* noise, but they are not especially vocal birds, giving an occasional subdued *quack*.

Shoveler

Sparrow

Mostly autumn to spring, widespread.

Male

Female

53 cm. 600-900 g.
see Mallard, page 38.

Pochard

Aythya ferina

Pochard

Sparrow

Thinly spread.

Pochards are inevitably linked with the more boldly-patterned Tufted Duck (page 48), as the two are so oft seen together and inhabit much the same kinds of place In most of Europe, Pochards are much scarcer as breeding birds than Tufted Ducks, and require denser cover at the edges of pools if they are to nest – so non breeding flocks are the most familiar. Males are obviou even at a distance, pale in the middle and dark at both ends, with deep chestnut-red heads that glow in good light. Females have the same long, low shape and neat. tapered bill, but look browner, less pure grey, and thei heads are dark liver-brown with paler faces. Unlike Tufted Ducks, they have grey wings with a paler centra panel, and no white stripe.

Pochards seem to live easy, lazy lives but become mo active at night: by day, they have a sleepy existence, bobbing about in groups, heads tucked back, sleeping one eye at a time. The male's eye is a lovely ruby-red.

Like other diving ducks, they are usually quiet birds and never 'quack': the typical call is a low, gruff growl In spring, though, males get together and display with rhythmic head movements, making much more interesting, almost sensuous calls, quiet but musical, lil a nasal, cooing, *ahh-ooh*.

Male

Female

49 cm. 600-1,200 g.
see Scaup and Tufted Duck, pages 50 and 48.

Tufted Duck

Aythya fuligula

This is a diving duck: it plunges from the surface as it swims, rather than diving from the air, or feeding out o dry land. It's common everywhere and mostly found o fresh water. It can be watched on park lakes, or floode gravel pits: like the Mallard, it is comfortable in the presence of people.

In some favoured places, such as the Ijsselmeer in The Netherlands, Tufted Ducks can be found in tens of thousands, but usually you might expect a few hundred a large reservoir or pit, often mixed with Pochards. Mal Tufteds are black and white, with a little dangling tassel the back of the head. In summer, they look like the fema dark chocolate brown, with grey bills, grey legs and lon white stripes on the wings. There is often a smudge of white under the tail, and a white mark beside the bill, bu the latter is less extensive than on a female Scaup.

Tufted Ducks are not excessively shy birds that nee careful stalking: you can often get surprisingly close. What you lose in the romance and inspiration of a wi bird, you gain in the chance to see every detail. There something special about a bird – still a wild creature – that you can observe well enough to distinguish every feather, and the glint in its gleaming yellow eye.

Tufted Duck

Sparrow

Almost everywhere, if habitat suitable.

Male

Female

47 cm. 350-950 g.
see Pochard page 46.

Scaup

Sparrow

Autumn to spring.

Scaup

Aythya marila

Scaup are lovely big sea ducks, with a liking for wide sandy bays and outer estuaries in winter. Here they feed small groups, occasionally larger flocks of a hundred or two, diving under to find food, or resting for long period on the surface, all heading one way, into the wind, looki rather round-backed and broad in the beam. In summer, they live far to the north in Europe and are unfamiliar birds. Even winter, flocks are mostly somewhat remote and little known to any but interested birdwatchers.

Winter males look black at both ends and pale in the middle, like drake Pochards crossed with Tufted Ducks with black heads and white flanks. The females are like larger, broader-bodied, heavier-billed female Tufted Ducks, but have a bigger blaze of white on the face an often a pale ear crescent. Young birds have less white and can be difficult to identify, but the size, shape and broader bill will help. Identifying these, and ruling out possible hybrid ducks, is a more advanced birdwatchin challenge, but good fun if you can scrutinise a big mix flock of diving ducks on a lake. Scaup are not often found on freshwater in such flocks, but one or two mig turn up to keep the inland birdwatcher happy and test his observation skills.

Male

Juvenile

51 cm. 850-1300 g.
see Tufted Duck, page 48.

Eider

Somateria mollissima

Everyone used to know of this bird because of eiderdown, the natural insulation material harvested from Eiders' nests, plucked by the ducks from their own bodies. These days, perhaps, the connection is not such common knowledge.

Eiders are sea ducks, big and heavy, yet amongst the fastest of birds in direct flight. They have long bills and wedge-shaped heads, which help to distinguish the brown females from other ducks, such as Mallards, at a distance. When they sleep, they often cock their short, square tails. Close up, you can see that the female Eider is barred cross-wise all over, rather than streaked lengthwise. In summer, they often paddle about with their ducklings among weedy rocks close to the shore, allowing close views. They can be wonderfully trusting.

The male is resplendent in black and white, set off by salmon-pink and pale green, unexpectedly dark below and white on top. In summer, however, and in immature stages, the male has a more irregular piebald appearance that can be confusing: then, the shape is a help, as is the tendency of Eiders to gather in long, lazy flocks on sheltered estuaries and bays close to the shore. They are rare on fresh water.

Winter and spring displays involve rhythmic posturing and deep, cooing, moaning calls.

Eider

Sparrow

All year.

Male

Female

cm. 1,900-2,800 g.
o see Mallard, page 38.

Long-tailed Duck

Clangula hyemalis

Long-tailed Duck

Sparrow

Autumn to spring.

Many people see their first Long-tailed Duck as a lone straggler on some inland water, there for a day or two but soon moving on. Such birds are usually immatures patchy plumages, identified by their stocky shape, stubbl bills and bulbous heads with various dark patches on th crown, cheek and chin.

In their element, Long-tailed Ducks are much more impressive, being found in flocks on the sea, often far offshore, but sometimes close in, on sandy bays or at the mouth of some northern estuary. These flocks are lively and often noisy: the birds make a chorus of yodelling, clanging notes, something like *aa-aa-ardl-ow*. Males posture and pose, challenging each other with raised hea and tails, while excited females look on with interest.

These winter drakes are fabulous creatures in white, pale grey and dark chocolate brown, a combination tha creates a strange appearance at times, one that can be difficult to grasp on a bird bobbing about on a rough se Summer birds are darker, with white faces. Males have pink band on the short bill, and long, whippy central ta feathers. Unlike Pintails, they do not graze on grass or estuarine mudflats, and the breast is dark, not white: on the long tail bears any real similarity to a Pintail's.

Male

Female

-45 cm. 500 g.
so see Pintail, page 40.

Common & Velvet Scoters

Melanitta nigra and *Melanitta fusca*

The **Common Scoter** is an almost exclusively marine duck except for when it nests. It breeds in the north but spends much of the year on the sea in large flocks. Even in summer there are many in favoured feeding areas, such as the larger bays of the Irish Sea and around north-east Scotland and the mouth of the Baltic.

The great majority of these will be Common Scoters, but a few Velvet Scoters can usually be found among them in more northerly flocks. Mostly, these flocks are well offshore – you won't see them unless you search. From a low vantage point, over a choppy sea, you may see little more than a line of birds in flight.

The **Velvet Scoter** is larger than the Common, and bulkier, with a rather flatter forehead profile helping to distinguish it. Both sexes have a broad rectangular panel of white at the back of each wing, but this can be hidden on a swimming bird. Only when a flock gets up and flies off, low over the waves, do the Velvets amongst them become obvious and these white rectangles sing out.

Velvet Scoters breed in the far north of Europe and Asia, and in winter flocks will usually be a small minority among other wildfowl. Nevertheless, Common Scoter flocks, from late summer on through the autumn and winter, are worth checking for the scarcer birds. Now and then, a Velvet Scoter will appear inland, on some reservoir or flooded pit

Common Scoter

Sparrow

Localized, off coasts.

Male
Velvet Scoter

Female Velvet
Scoter

ale
nmon
ter

ale
nmon
ter

Velvet Scoter

Sparrow

nmon Scoter: 46-51 cm. 700-1,300 g.
et Scoter: 53-59 cm. 1,000-1,500 g.
 see Eider, page 52.

Coasts, autumn and
winter.

Goldeneye

Bucephala clangula

Some ducks are familiar to everyone, but not this one.
isn't rare, but it is shy and it appears over much of
Europe only in the winter, coming down from the nort
It likes larger lakes, flooded pits and reservoirs, or the
sea. In upland areas, where pools are apt to be deep, c
and acidic, the goldeneye may often be the only duck
on the water.

It feeds with a passion for much of the day and it is
often difficult to know how many there are on a patch
water: for much of the time, most of them are
submerged. If disturbed, all may stay on the surface at
once, or fly off on loudly whistling wings, surprising t
watcher with the true size of the flock. At other times,
Goldeneyes take a rest, flying to some undisturbed par
of the lake to sleep away an hour or two in a tight flo
each with the rather long tail cocked. When feeding, t
keep the tail flat on the water and look short-bodied a
round-backed, with large, bulbous heads and short bi
Winter males are striking in shining snow-white and
black, with a big white face spot, while females are da
birds, grey with a brown head, the details often hard t
see at long range against cold, grey, rippled water.

Goldeneye

Sparrow

Widespread in
winter.

Male

Female

50 cm. 500-1,200 g.
 see Tufted Duck, Smew, pages 48 and 60.

Smew

Mergellus albellus

In most countries, such as England, the Smew is scarce and exciting to see, a winter bird usually found in ones and twos or, at most as small groups in single figures, on gravel pits and reservoirs. Elsewhere, though, especially the Netherlands, there are winter flocks of hundreds, even thousands, and these transform anyone's view of the Smew. They are active, lively, constantly busy, bold birds, marvellous to watch. Like the other 'sawbills' (see Merganser and Goosander) they have beaks with serrated edges and dive for food.

Winter males, although marked with delicate black linear patterns, are strikingly white, matched only by the bigger, much pinker, Goosander, and the lumpier, black-headed Goldeneye. The white plumage of a Smew is faintly yellow-tinged and its flanks are pale grey, whereas the Goldeneye is a stark icy-white, including the flanks. Smew sit low in the water and look small headed, unless the loose, fuzzy crest is raised momentarily in display or aggression, or simple curiosity. This reveals a black nape patch, to complement the black spot on the face between the eye and bill.

Females are much greyer birds, with ginger-brown heads, white throats and white wing patches. The Merganser and Goosander have similar basic colours, but have longer, slender bills that are red, not grey, as well as orange legs.

Smew

Sparrow

Winter on coasts and (mainly coastal) fresh water.

Male

Female

43 cm. 500 g.
see Goldeneye, Goosander, pages 58 and 64.

Red-breasted Merganser

Mergus serrator

It is pointless arguing which of the diving ducks is mos attractive, but the drake Red-breasted Merganser is certainly both elegantly shaped and prettily patterned. has that extra flamboyance afforded by the upstanding spiky crest, often more or less split into two clumps. T Goosander has a thicker, drooping, more rounded cres A drake Merganser also has a dark breast and grey flanks, unlike the pink-white overall on a Goosander.

Mergansers have longer, slimmer bills than Goosanders, with a faintly upswept, almost grinning effect, and brighter, more scarlet or vermilion in colou The grey-bodied female is less pure grey than a female Goosander, slightly tinged browner, but the most usefu difference is in the head and neck pattern: a Goosande has a solid brown head and sharp white chin patch, while a Merganser has a blurred, ginger-brown head, blending into a soft, dull pale throat.

Mergansers breed near rivers and coasts in the nort and west, but are generally much more marine than Goosanders, often forming flocks in sheltered inlets an bays. Pairs frequently display through the winter, the males pointing their slender bills into the air and archi their backs in ritualised posturing, then taking off and flying fast and low around the estuary.

Red-breasted Merganser

Sparrow

All year on N and
W coasts; S coasts
in winter.

Female

Male

m. 850-1,300 g.
see Goosander, page 64.

Goosander

Sparrow

All year in N and W.
Winter visitor to
lowlands.

Goosander

Mergus merganser

Most birds, are especially fine close up, of course, but there are exceptions. Go to a large, bleak reservoir in winter, and you're likely to see several hundred anonymous looking ducks bobbing on the chop. Noth special. But if you take the trouble to scan carefully as far out as possible, you might be lucky enough to see handful of Goosanders. Even at long range, the males salmon-pink – long, lithe, large birds with black heads without doubt, an exciting find.

Goosanders nest in tree holes beside upland rivers lakes, and move to larger, often lowland, lakes in win as well as to the coast. They are controversial because they eat fish – as they have done for millions of years The male is flushed (to a varying degree) with pink, h head black with a deep green gloss. The hooked, serrated bill is dark plum-red. The female is clear pal grey, with a white breast sharply contrasted against a dark brown head, and a small white throat patch, un the smudgy colours of the browner Red-breasted Merganser, which also has a fuzzy crest instead of a thick, bushy crest at the nape.

Goosanders fly quite often, although perfectly adap for life on water. In the air, they look thick-bodied, bu torpedo-shaped, with relatively small black and white wings set well back.

Female

Male

9 cm. 1,250-1,900 g.
see Red-breasted Merganser, page 62.

Red/Willow Grouse

Lagopus lagopus

In spring, a male Red Grouse stands in a thick tussock heather, on a small rise in an otherwise featureless mo and makes his presence known to the other grouse around him. His calls are hard, gritty, abrupt croaks a cascades of rhythmic, rattling notes, ideally suited to these harsh surroundings. He looks as if he might be sculpted from a fine, polished piece of dark granite, inseparable from heather and gritty moorland.

In the UK and Ireland, the bird has all-dark wings, and is called the Red Grouse, while the mainland European form or race is known as the Willow Grous and has white wings, like a Ptarmigan. On the Europe mainland it becomes a white bird in winter, while the Red Grouse remains unchanged all year round.

Grouse are superficially chicken- or partridge-like birds, with short, feathered legs and short, thick, hook beaks for dealing with heather shoots and seeds and small, tough berries. They live in small groups, often hidden in the heather until almost trodden on when th go off with a long, staccato rattle of alarm, finishing i several well separated notes, like *go-back go-back go-b back bak bak*. They are fine birds, paid too little atten by birdwatchers, perhaps, as they are so inextricably associated with expensive, exclusive shooting.

Red/Willow Grouse

Sparrow

All year.

Red Grouse

Willow Grouse

cm. 600-700 g.
see Grey Partridge, page 72.

Black Grouse

Tetrao tetrix

High on the edge of a heathery moor, where green
pastures lie between stone walls and a scrubby wood of
birch and larch peters out against a boggy hollow, Black
Grouse gather in spring to display at a traditional site
called a lek. Inconspicuous females look on, quietly
choosing a mate.

The fights are more for show than for real, all puff and
bluster, but the birds look big and impressive, and spread
curiously lyre-shaped tails as wide as they will go. They
croon with repeated patterns of pigeon-like bubbling, and
leap into the air with loud, sneezing sounds. You can see
their steaming breath on a frosty morning.

These are among Europe's most showy birds, as big as
a large cockerel, steely-blue and black, with white under
the tail, white wing bars and a red wattle over each eye.
Females look more like pale Red Grouse, or female
Pheasants, but have notched tails and a hint of a pale
wing stripe.

As farming has intensified, woods have been cleared
and moorland has degenerated, Black Grouse have
declined. In lowland areas, such as the Netherlands and
Britain's New Forest, they have disappeared from ancient
heathland. Still, in winter, when they may stand out on
short grass, it is possible, in places, to come across a few
and they are obvious and easy to see in such a situation

Black Grouse (male)

Black Grouse (female)

Sparrow

All year in suitable
habitat.

Male

Female

-55 cm. 750-1,400 g.
o see Capercaillie, page 70.

Capercaillie
Tetrao urogallus

Capercaillie (male)

Capercaillie (female)

Sparrow

All year in Scandinavia; rarely in Scotland, Pyrenees, Alps.

Extensive tracts of old, undisturbed pine with an abundance of juniper, heather, bilberry, crowberry and cowberry beneath, adjacent to areas of damp bog, also well supplied with heather shoots and berries, makes ideal Capercaillie terrain. Anywhere else, it struggles to survive, and the species is declining in most of its European range, under pressure from development, disturbance and perhaps from increased predation. The changing climate may also play a part. Cold, wet weather in early summer seems to be lethal for Capercaillie chicks.

Another cause of Capercaillie deaths is the spread of tall deer fencing: thin, taught wires at just the height a Capercaillie likes to fly when returning to its woodland home from a foraging trip on a nearby bog. Capercaillie have no chance when they strike such a fence at speed.

These old pines woods, in flat river basins or on the slopes of majestic mountain ranges, are inspiring places full of colour and life, and the Capercaillie is one of the scarce inhabitants. It is difficult to glimpse, even though large. It is turkey sized, the male huge and dark, with a broad, rounded tail, the female slimmer, browner, with complex patterns of black, cream and rufous, and a similar, rounded tail. Not even the Black Grouse comes close in size; and a hen Pheasant is much longer tailed.

Female

Male

87 cm. 1,500-4,400 g.
‎ ‎ see Black Grouse, page 68.

Grey & Red-legged Partridge

Perdix perdix and *Alectoris rufa*

On a spring morning, in un-modernised farmland, the creaky-gate call of a Grey Partridge remains a familiar and traditional feature. In intensively-farmed land, whe flowers and insects have been drastically reduced, the partridges have gone: their chicks, especially, need sma insects if they are to thrive. Because partridges are routinely shot for sport, many farmers will try to help them increase, and are paid to grow sharply-defined strips of non-commercial plants around fields.

Red-legged Partridges are Southern European birds, introduced to Northern Europe and Britain long ago. Originally, they were birds of rough, unkempt, heathla slopes and warm, even semi-arid environments.

Both are rounded, chicken-like birds, but with short tails held low, short legs and small bills. The Grey is more streaked, with an orange-brown face and greyer underparts. A Red-legged is plain above, much more heavily barred across the flanks, and has a striking wh face surrounded by black. And, naturally, it has red leg but these are not so immediately striking. Red-legs do odd things, too, compared with the Grey Partridge, su as perching on top of walls, barns, even sometimes houses. The Grey is much more of a rural bird. Nevertheless, both overlap considerably and can be see too, on less obvious places such as coastal sand dunes.

Grey Partridge

Sparrow

Most of Europe, all year.

Grey Partridge

Red-legged Partridge

Red-legged Partridge

Sparrow

Grey Partridge: 30 cm. 320-430 g.
Red-legged Partridge: 34 cm. 400-540 g.
Also see Quail, Red Grouse, Pheasant, pages 74, 66 and 76.

Mainly Spain,
France, Britain.

Quail & Corncrake

Coturnix coturnix and *Crex crex*

These two unrelated species share two characteristics: both are usually disembodied voices, heard from the depths of tall crop; and both migrate to Africa for the winter.

The **Quail** is widespread but comes and goes, numbers varying from year to year, especially in fringe areas of its range such as Britain. This is no surprise, considering how many are illegally trapped in spring on Mediterranean islands, and how many are netted every autumn on the North African coast. Sadly, too, these same nets catch **Corncrakes**, and the Corncrake has already disappeared from most of its range over the past century.

Quails like cereal fields but are undone by their replacement with subsidised rape or some other unsuitable crop. Corncrakes need early spring cover, such as nettles, followed by a late summer crop of hay. They are unable to survive in the face of intensive grass growing for silage, abetted by modern machinery.

The Quail calls a quick, rhythmic, liquid *whit-wit-it* ('kiss-me-quick') and the bird itself is exceptionally hard to see. The Corncrake rasps out a hard, wholly unmusical *crrik-crrik* or *crark-ark*, dry and brittle from a distance, reverberating rattle at close range. Quails look like tiny, streaky, slim-winged partridges with striped heads, while Corncrakes are more like streaky-brown, pale-beaked Moorhens in shape and action, with bright rufous wings

Quail

Sparrow

April to September.

Quail

Corncrake

Corncrake

Sparrow

April to September.

Quail: 18 cm. 80-140 g.
Corncrake: 30 cm. 120-200 g.
Also see Grey Partridge, page 72.

Pheasant

Phasianus colchicus

This is the most familiar game bird in Europe, originall[y] an Asian species, introduced for shooting all over Euro[pe] and in many other parts of the world. It is easy to see, marching across fields and parkland in the open, although at dusk Pheasants fly up into trees to roost.

The males, especially, are obvious, big and bright, usually deep chestnut-brown with dark, glossy green heads (and often white neck rings) and long, stiff, tapered tails. Females have a similar shape, but less extravagantly long tails, and are pale buff-brown with dark mottles.

Millions of pheasants are released each year and swarm, semi-tame, through the fields, waiting to be sh[ot] but 'wild' ones live in the edges of forests and wander into reed beds and other areas of dense vegetation, wh[ere] they are more secretive. They scare more people than a[ny] other bird, as they have the habit of sitting tight and 'exploding' from the undergrowth with a loud flurry o[f] wings and raucous calls, when almost underfoot. They suffer severely from cars as well as shotgun pellets: nex[t] time you're on a country road or lane, count the squashed Pheasants.

Pheasant

Sparrow

Most of Europe, all year.

Male

Female

90 cm. 750-1,800 g.
see Partridges, page 72.

Black- & Red- throated Divers

Gavia arctica and *Gavia stellata*

Divers, supposedly primitive birds, are more elegantly perfected to their own specialised way of life than almost any other. Long-bodied, torpedo-shaped, powered by lobed toes on short, strong legs right at the back, like a ship's propeller, they work wonderfully well under water and sit, backs almost awash, beautifully upon it. On land, they are hopeless; in the air, powerful and fast in a straight line, but they need plenty of time and space in which to turn.

The **Red-throated**, which breeds on small Scottish lochs and feeds in the sea, is the least striking, brown with a finely-striped grey head and dark red throat in summer; in winter it is brown, speckled white, with the white of its face spreading above the eye. Its chief feature is a slender upturned bill, held pointing upwards a touch.

The **Black-throated**, in winter, is more solidly dark above, its white face less extensive, and its pale bill is a horizontal, evenly tapered dagger. In summer, when it retreats to larger Scottish lochs with islands or specially provided rafts, it becomes a bird of impossibly perfect pattern. Its black back has discrete areas of white chequering, its head is plush velvet-grey, blacker around the eye, and its throat purple-black above a necklace of white spots; the sides of the white breast have wonderfully drawn, tapered lines of black and white.

Black-throated Diver

Sparrow

Coasts in winter.

Black-throated Diver, summer

Black-throated Diver, winter

Red-throated Diver, winter

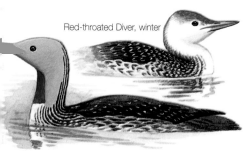

Red-throated Diver, summer

Red-throated Diver

Sparrow

Coasts in winter.

ck-throated: 70 cm. 1,300-3,400 g.
d-throated: 60 cm. 1,000-1,600 g.
 see Great Crested Grebe, page 84.

Great Northern Dive

Gavia immer

Speeding by on the tide at the mouth of an estuary is a lo
shape, water washing over its broad back before it rolls
forward into a long dive. It could be a Cormorant – or is
more exciting? Instead of the Cormorant's hook-tipped
beak, this big diver sports a dramatic dagger of a bill.
Compared with the smaller Black-throated Diver, the
winter Great Northern has a browner (less black) back,
variably barred paler on immature birds, a blacker nape
and a blackish band each side of the base of the neck.
Otherwise, it looks much the same – dark on top, silky
white beneath.

In spring and summer, the Great Northern is rare in
Europe, breeding in Iceland and the Arctic. In summer
plumage, it is an exciting red-letter-day treat, most likely
be seen in Scotland's northern isles. It is then a magnifice
sight, scarcely equalled in its dramatic pattern of close
white chequering over the upper parts and a striped colla
of white lines below the green-black head.

In Western Europe, the Great Northern Diver is
basically a coastal bird, but now and then one or two
turn up far inland on some large lake or reservoir, and
may stay for weeks if left in peace. They dive
wonderfully well, but in the air, although powerful
enough, have little manoeuvrability and fly with their
long necks drooping and big feet trailing behind.

Great Northern Diver

Sparrow

Coasts in winter.

Winter

Summary

cm. 1,600-4,000 g.
see Black-throated Diver, Cormorant, pages 78 and 96.

Little Grebe

Tachybaptus ruficollis

Little Grebe

Sparrow

All year except in
highest places.

Smaller by some way than a Moorhen or a Coot, this
the smallest freshwater bird likely to be seen swimming
on a river or pond or, from autumn to late winter, even
out in the middle of a big reservoir. Sometimes, on a
warm late summer day, peculiar little ringing and trilling
notes can be heard from large flocks of brown, moulting
ducks. They can't be pinned down to individual birds,
and these are in fact Little Grebes holding their watery
conversations. In spring, territorial males burst out with
long, loud, whinnying trills.

Little Grebes eat small aquatic creatures, caught under
water in true grebe fashion. They are brilliant divers and
disappear for what seems like ages, only to reappear far
away, or to come up under the overhanging vegetation of
a bank, escaping detection altogether. They seem nervous
and shy, yet allow quite a close approach, so you can
often get a clear view. In winter they are dull brown, with
a darker cap and paler face, and a yellowish-white spot
by the bill. In summer, the head and neck become bright
deep rufous-red and black, the bill spot much more
striking. Although not the most colourful of the grebes
display they can spread out the feathers around the
minute tail and flanks to reveal a warm, bright, orange-
buff. Young ones have black stripes on the head.

Summer

Winter

29 cm. 100-290 g.
o see Black-necked Grebe, page 88.

Great Crested Grebe

Podiceps cristatus

The biggest of the grebes, the Great Crested tends to mislead on a large lake, often far out, neck held upright and gleaming white, looking as big as a diver or at least a Mallard. Close up, it seems small, round-bodied, with no tail to speak of. It is the size of a medium duck, with a long, slim neck that can be erect or withdrawn, and a pointed, dagger-like bill.

Grebes' feet have broad lobes along the toes, folding back like a leaf, so that a forward stroke underwater gives no resistance, but a backward stroke offers strong forwards propulsion, whether the bird is swimming on the surface or under water, where it is a fast and powerful pursuer of fish.

Great Crested Grebe

Large fish are brought to the surface to be turned and swallowed. Grebes also swallow small feathers, which give a tough lining to the stomach to protect against fish bone. You may see parents feeding feathers to their stripe-head chicks, which often ride on the adults' backs.

Black-headed Gull

Red-necked Grebes (page 86) have smoky-grey fore necks and bigger black caps than Great Crested, while the other grebes are much smaller. Divers are much longer-bodied than grebes. Great Cresteds have unique facial adornments from late winter to autumn, used in ritualised displays in spring. They fly little, with legs and necks drooped, showing much white on the wing.

Not in N Scotland.

Winter

Winter

51 cm. 600-1,400 g.
see Red-necked Grebe, page 86.

Red-necked Grebe

Podiceps grisegena

One of the larger grebes, the Red-necked is big-headed, thick-necked and stocky, with a long, rather heavy bill. lacks the snaky elegance of the Great Crested and often looks more like a big Slavonian or Black-necked Grebe winter, more black, grey and white than the brownish Great Crested, with a dusky face and, uniquely, a patch of yellow on the bill. In summer, it develops a neat, shin black cap, rounded rather than crested at the back, and grey face, whiter around the eye, but often very dark on the cheek. This patch contrasts sharply with the dull, deep red of the neck and breast (a Great Crested alway has a bright white front).

In this handsome breeding plumage it is found on larg rivers and associated marshes right across Europe, but most commonly in the east, for example on the Danub Delta. In the west, it is widely scattered and scarce in summer, occasionally nesting far outside its usual range conditions are right, but is much better known as a winter bird. Small numbers move on to sheltered coast and estuaries, sometimes arriving in August or Septemb still in breeding colours, a treat for birdwatchers, who normally see it as a dull, dark bird, if at all. It is a discovery to brighten a cold, dark winter day.

Red-necked Grebe

Sparrow

Breeds N Europe.

Winter

Winter

46 cm. 500-1,000 g.
see Great Crested Grebe, page 84.

Black-necked & Slavonian Grebes

Podiceps nigricollis and *Podiceps aurit*

Grebes are fascinating birds, all but tail-less, round and densely-feathered, their legs too far back to be of practi use on land, equipped with long, broadly-lobed toes. In short, these are water birds through and through, so brilliantly adapted to their aquatic environment – they spend almost as much time under water as on top – tha they have surrendered any pretence of being at home ashore or in the air. These two small grebes, barely Moorhen-sized, are colourful in summer, but black, whi and lead-grey in winter, except for red-currant eyes.

Black-necked Grebe

The **Slavonian Grebe** is generally the more northerly bird. In summer, its neck, breast and flanks are orange-red; the black head has a horizontal wedge of gold abo each eye. The **Black-necked** has coppery flanks, but is black on the breast, neck and pointed head, with a fan yellow drooping from each cheek.

Sparrow

In winter, when both are more widespread, but neve numerous, the Slavonian has a sharper look about it, with a smooth black cap above a white cheek, a faint whitish mark before the eye, and a straight bill with a pale tip. The Black-necked is smudgier, its crown still more peaked, the cheeks greyer with a whitish 'hook' above each ear, and a much greyer neck. Its beak is da all over and tilts upwards a little towards the tip.

Coasts in winter.

Black-necked Grebe, winter

Black-necked Grebe, spring

Slavonian Grebe, winter

Slavonian Grebe, summer

Slavonian Grebe

Sparrow

Coasts in winter.

Black-necked: 30 cm. 250-400 g.
Slavonian: 35 cm. 375-470 g.
Also see Red-necked Grebe, page 86.

Fulmar

Fulmarus glacialis

The sea offers many pleasures to the birdwatcher. On rugged coasts, with rocky headlands and little sheltered bays, stony storm beaches backed by dunes and cliffs, there will often be steep, slippery green slopes dotted with spots of white. These animated white spots will be Fulmars, each on its single egg laid in a shallow earthy depression. (The Guillemot, by contrast, stands in long, regimented lines on cliff ledges. See page 228.) When the male reappears from a foraging expedition out to sea, the two set up a duet of manic witch-like cackling and throaty coughs that echo across the water, without melody, but hugely evocative.

Fulmar

Fulmars look superficially like gulls but, on land, they barely move and can't stand. On water they swim with tails cocked up and heads high. In the air they are at their best, flying with stiffly fluttering wings and long, sweeping glides, all the better if there is wind. Unlike most gulls, their grey wings have dull grey tips, with no black, and, while the large white head is obvious, the broad rump and tail are grey. Their short, squat, hooked bills have a curious structure of plates and a double tube on top which does service as nostrils: Fulmars are tubenoses, related to the shearwaters and the magnificent albatrosses of the southern oceans.

Black-headed Gull

Commonest in N.

-50 cm. 600-1,000 g.
o see Herring Gull, page 214.

Manx Shearwater

Puffinus puffinus

Manx Shearwater breeding colonies, which are nearly a on islands, are, perhaps surprisingly, not the best places to see this bird. Some colonies in Scotland and Wales have tens of thousands of pairs, but in order to avoid predatory gulls, the birds come to land only in darknes even avoiding a full moon. Shearwaters are almost helpless on land, scuttling quickly into their deep nestin burrows using feet, bill and half-open wings. Meanwhi the air is full of the caterwauling calls of birds locating their mates.

At sea it is a different story. Here, shearwaters are in their element, and it is best to watch for them from a long headland. 'Shearwater' is well deserved: they shea close to the waves on stiff wings, tilting over to show t black upperside, then the silky white beneath. Usually small parties drift together, but not closely co-ordinate each bird takes its individual, erratic course. Where the are many come together, a large area of sea may be dotted with the small, wavering, cross-shaped birds. In calm weather, they must flap more often and their actio is a distinctive flap-flap-glide. If the wind is fierce, they ride it on longer, bounding glides, sailing fast downwin then veering steeply against it to gain height, ready for the next long downward slide. They are perfectly adapted for their long life at sea.

Manx Shearwater

Black-headed Gull

Spring to autumn.
Breeds on
remote islands.

38 cm. 340-500 g.
see Fulmar, page 90.

Gannet

Morus bassanus

The largest North Atlantic seabird, the Gannet is handsome and dramatic. On its breeding ledges in summer, it packs in tight, each nesting bird within a stretched beak's length of the next: any trespass by an adult or chick draws a vicious response from its neighbours. Overhead, off-duty birds sail in the breeze, chequering a blue sky with inky black and vivid white.

Out at sea, the Gannet is a master, using wind and air currents over the waves to travel great distances with little effort. From many western headlands, Gannets may be seen passing by the hour in long, thin processions between feeding grounds and nesting sites. Of the latter there are few, mostly on offshore islands.

Feeding Gannets spy fish from aloft and, depending on conditions, plunge in from a height or dive at an angle from lower down, either way entering with a splash at speed. When fish shoals are close to the surface, diving Gannets pepper the sea, creating a magnificent spectacle.

While adult Gannets are spotlessly white, except for black wing tips and a golden-buff head, juveniles are blackish with paler spots, and immature birds, for the next couple of years, look piebald, getting whiter with age. Most of these young birds spend time in warmer waters off the coast of West Africa until they are old enough to breed.

Gannet

Black-headed Gull

Mostly N and W in summer and autumn.

Juvenile

Adults

39 cm. 2.5-3.5 kg.
see Great Black-backed Gull, page 216.

Cormorant

Phalacrocorax carbo

Cormorants are devil birds to some people, the 'black plague' of the angling press, because they catch fish, ar are very good at it, too. The rights and wrongs of culli Cormorants, against scientific evidence, have been long debated. Cormorants are not welcome at inland fisheri

They are, in their big, ugly way, fine birds. The thick, hooked bill and bare facial skin (brightly coloured in spring); the neatly-outlined, scaly feathering on the back and wings; the bold white throat; long, fine white plume on the head and the square white thigh patches in spring make for a handsome effect, if also somewhat prehistoric

Cormorants often stand on a buoy, or pier, or moor boat, with their wings half open. It is usually said that this is drying their wings, although sharp eyed people note that they also do this in the rain. Maybe the habit something to do with aiding digestion after a meal of cold, slippery, scaly fish.

In the water, they swim with their backs almost awa and hold their heads tilted upwards, a useful indication that you are not watching a Great Northern Diver, wh a young Cormorant may otherwise resemble.

Cormorants nest colonially, on cliffs or in trees, whe they make enormous stick nests like those of Grey Herons, which might share the same clump of trees.

Cormorant

Black-headed Gull

Widespread,
especially in winter.

Immature

Adults

cm. 2.5-3.5 kg.
see Shag, page 98.

Shag

Phalacrocorax aristotelis

The Shag is a smaller, more sinuous version of the Cormorant but the two can be difficult to separate. The Shag is much more restricted to the sea. It likes rocky coasts and feeds in dangerous surf that seems likely to dash its brains out on the rocks. It plunges under, typically with a little leap clear of the water as it goes. The Cormorant has a smoother forward roll as befits its greater weight.

Shags may feed in large flocks, sometimes hundreds together, whereas Cormorants are usually in smaller groups. Close up, you may discern the thinner bill and steeper forehead of the Shag, and snakier neck. Adult Shags never have a white chin, but do have a yellow throat patch. Young Shags are browner underneath than the white-breasted young Cormorants, with a pale throat.

Shags nest on sea cliffs and in caves (not in trees, which Cormorants often do) and create vast areas of splashed whitewash by the end of the season, so they are not difficult to find. Adults are black with a green gloss and, in spring, sport little, upstanding crests on the foreheads, doing their best, with what little they have, to look beautiful. Depending on your point of view, they may succeed: a mixture of elegance with clumsiness, and a lovely pattern of black feather edges on green.

Shag

Black-headed Gull

Rocky coasts.
Rare inland.

Juvenile

Adult

cm. 1,500-2,200 g.
see Cormorant, page 96.

Bittern

Botaurus stellaris

A Bittern is a bird of the reeds: it lives in reeds, and it can look like reeds. When alarmed, it stands still, point its bill upwards, and may gently sway: the streaks on it neck look exactly like stems of dried reed.

All this works because the Bittern lives its entire life beds of reeds. Only occasionally does one fly over the reed tops, except in spring, when males may do so to look over and perhaps mark out their territories, and when pairs return to the nest from distant fishing place Otherwise, the Bittern mooches about on foot, on the mud under the reeds or clambering along, grasping several stems at a time in its long, slender toes.

Bitterns eat fish, so must have access to water, from within the reed bed. A Bittern-friendly reed bed has to contain open ditches, or sufficient depth of water throughout. The problem with reed beds is that they te to dry out – fine if new reed beds are being created elsewhere, but modern land management, with rivers a marshes held tight behind banks and flood defences, do not allow that. Marshes have to be managed artificially for Bitterns to survive.

You may not see a Bittern in its secretive world, but spring you might hear one, giving a deep, hollow, far-carrying *whoomp!*, the Bittern's famous boom.

Bittern

Sparrow

All year, but very sparse.

cm. 850-1,900 g.
o see Grey Heron, page 104.

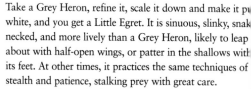

Little Egret

Egretta garzetta

Take a Grey Heron, refine it, scale it down and make it pu
white, and you get a Little Egret. It is sinuous, slinky, snak
necked, and more lively than a Grey Heron, likely to leap
about with half-open wings, or patter in the shallows with
its feet. At other times, it practices the same techniques of
stealth and patience, stalking prey with great care.

It used to be a 'Mediterranean' bird, although it was als
found widely in areas such as north-western France, but in
recent decades it has spread north dramatically. In Britain,
from a great rarity it became rare but regular, then
established itself around the south coast, and now it breed
often in Grey Heronries, in respectable numbers.

Little Egrets like soft, muddy marshes with creeks,
sheltered estuaries and river mouths, and shallow brackish
or fresh water pools close to the sea. They penetrate inlan
along river valleys and appear on floods, gravel pits and a
the edges of reservoirs, but such exposed places are
occupied rather briefly.

This is not the only white egret. The Cattle Egret usuall
has a yellow bill, not a black one, and paler legs, or all-da
legs without the yellow feet that distinguish the Little Egre
The Little Egret has black legs with yellow toes. The Grea
White Egret (a vagrant but increasingly often in North-
western Europe) is bigger, not always easy to distinguish,
but has a longer, heavier, often yellow bill.

Little Egret

Sparrow

Widespread in S.
Now in N France
and in Britain.

58 cm. 450-600 g.

Grey Heron

Black-headed Gull

Not on high moors
or hills.

Grey Heron

Ardea cinerea

This big, impressive bird typifies stealth and application.
It stands motionless for long minutes, or strides slowly
forwards, in shallow water, on marshy ground, or among
weed-covered rocks at the edge of the sea, in search of
whatever might come its way. Fish form the bulk of its
prey, but anything from frogs and birds to rats, even
moles, may be snatched by the long, dagger-like bill.

Herons are sedate creatures and spend hours standing
in groups in open fields far from water. On the other
hand, a heronry in spring is a lively, noisy place. The
birds make big stick nests in the tops of trees, and there
a remarkable chorus of castanet rattles of their beaks and
raucous calls from adults and young. Birds arriving from
distant feeding grounds come in at a height and tumble
down, descending with a series of fast twists and turns.
These great birds, with their long, broad, arched wings
can even soar surprisingly well if they wish.

Adults seen close up are beautiful, with bold yellow
eyes, a long black crest from the back of the head, near
black chequering on the front of the white neck and
pointed, pale plumes on the back. Juveniles have dull
grey heads and necks but are otherwise similarly grey,
with blacker flight feathers.

-98 cm. 1,100-1,750 g.
so see Crane, page 152.

White Stork

Sparrow

Much of central and
S Europe.

White Stork

Ciconia ciconia

This is the early spring arrival perennially welcomed in towns and villages across mainland Europe. The White Stork most often nests on buildings or on poles, sometimes specially erected for it, in and around towns and villages. Sadly, although people still like them, the way they manage their land as farming becomes more intensive has meant harder times for the White Stork. It prefers damp fields and small pools, with long grass, patches of reed, clumps of rushes and the like, where it can find frogs, small rodents and other such food. Smooth, fertilised, herbicide-treated, uniform dry grass has little to offer. In consequence, storks are in decline over much of their range.

The huge white birds are a stirring sight, with their bills like enormous red daggers, marching slowly on long, red legs through a lush growth of colourful meadow and marsh plants. As Eastern Europe, especially succumbs to the subsidised, squeaky-clean ways of Western Europe, so these birds are becoming scarcer.

Storks nest in small groups as a rule, but isolated pairs may settle on a church tower or some such spot, building a huge nest of sticks that is visible from miles around. In the autumn they gather into flocks and head south, flying over the Mediterranean to Africa at the shortest crossing

105 cm. 3-4 kg.
o see Grey Heron, page 104.

Spoonbill

Sparrow

Rare in the UK.

Spoonbill
Platalea leucorodia

Few European birds have such specialised features that they might be called grotesque: perhaps the Spoonbill i one. A feeding Spoonbill walks slowly through shallow water, leaning forwards, its beak half open and half submerged. It sweeps the beak from side to side until it touches something – with luck a fish or shrimp – then snaps it shut. It seems an inefficient way of feeding, bu the big, rounded, flat-ended spoon of a bill is ideal for the job.

It walks like a human, with a long, even stride. Overall, it is white, except for some rich buff at the ba of the neck in spring. The bill is black, with a yellow ti (greyer on young birds, pink on very young ones), the legs black. Adults have a bushy, pineapple crest, which blows in the wind, or droops heavily over the nape.

Because Spoonbills need shallow water full of food, they are localized in Europe. The Netherlands has a fe colonies, and there are others in the south, especially ir Spain, and the far east of Europe, but in the north-wes Spoonbills are rare wanderers, most often seen in late summer and autumn. While easily seen and identified i their colonies, vagrants are an exciting find.

90 cm. 1,100-1,900 g.
see Little Egret, page 102.

Honey-buzzard

Pernis apivorus

Not a true buzzard, but looking very like one, this is a
migrant from Africa, arriving in north-western Europe in
spring and leaving via the shortest possible sea crossings i
autumn. The southern tip of Sweden, Gibraltar and the
Bosporus have the biggest concentrations.

Except when on migration, the Honey-buzzard is a
solitary bird and can be elusive, especially in areas such a
England and Scotland where the population is small and
breeding pairs are widely scattered. In late spring, a male
will advertise its presence by special display flights above
the nesting wood, sometimes rising steeply and clapping i
wings together over its back. Otherwise, they keep their
heads down, sitting deep within a wood, watching for
passing wasps and bees. These they follow to the nests,
which are then dug out with stout, hooked claws. Stiff,
bristly facial feathers provide some protection from sting
The bird probably also has a degree of immunity to the
angry insects' venom. It also eats grubs and wax from th
structure of the nest.

In flight, Honey-buzzards differ from buzzards in the
way they hold their wings, which are flat or drooped, no
raised in a V when soaring, and in the narrower head an
longer tail, which has three distinct dark bands. To ident
them you need to be a relatively advanced birdwatcher –
even the experienced sometimes find them difficult.

Honey-buzzard

Sparrow

Over much of Europe
but rare in Britain.

Dark bird

58 cm. 500-800 g.
see Buzzard, page 130.

Black Kite

Milvus migrans

Black Kite

Sparrow

March to October,
not Scandinavia
and UK.

Many birds of prey fly well, but kites take aerial brilliance to special heights – although usually to no great altitude. They don't need to fly fast, nor do they soar to great heights, but Black Kites can remain in the air for long periods with little effort, cover huge areas, and show great precision when chasing prey or dropping on to some scrap of dead meat. Nevertheless, anyone who has had a piece of food snatched from them by a Black Kite – in Africa, perhaps, where they can be very bold – will tell you that Black Kites are big, fast and intimidating and can deliver a real punch.

Black Kites arrive in Europe in spring from Africa. They are most at home in warm, dry areas in the south and hang around water, snatching dead fish from the surface. In Northern Europe, they are rare, in Britain elusive vagrants.

The Black Kite's long tail has a shallow notch, rather than the deeper V of a Red Kite's. The notch is only obvious when the tail is open, not when it is closed. The upper surfaces of the wings have pale bands from the body to the wrist joint. These are even brighter on a Red Kite, but help distinguish a Black Kite from the Marsh Harrier, which otherwise looks rather like a kite and can be surprisingly hard to rule out.

59 cm. 800-1,000 g.
see Marsh Harrier, Buzzard pages 120 and 130.

Red Kite

Milvus milvus

Red Kite

Sparrow

All year in S and W,
leaves N in winter.

As recently as the 1970s, the Red Kite in Britain was restricted to a handful of pairs breeding, often with little success, in mid Wales. Elsewhere in Britain it was an exceptionally rare vagrant, although centuries before it had been widespread. In much of the European mainland Red Kites had survived better: it was savage persecution that did for them in Britain, and cold, wet springs made Wales a less than perfect refuge in many years.

With protection, however, and not a little artificial feeding, Red Kites in Wales have boomed to unexpected numbers, and spread a little in range. At the same time, artificial reintroduction projects have returned them to several parts of England and Scotland, with Northern Ireland to follow. Hundreds of pairs now nest successfully where recently there were none.

This wonderful conservation success story has brought the elegance of a big, colourful, majestic bird of prey to the doorsteps – almost literally – of thousands of people. The Red Kite is longer-winged than a Buzzard, with a longer, forked, rusty tail, big white patches under each wing, broad creamy bands across the shoulders and a pale greyish head: it uses its tail as a rudder in flight and achieves a degree of aerial agility rarely matched by other birds of prey. It feeds mostly on dead rabbits and sheep in the hills, but can catch small birds and mammals.

64 cm. 800-1,000 g.
see Black Kite, page 112.

White-tailed Eagle

Haliaeetus albicilla

White-tailed Eagle

Sparrow

Norwegian White-tailed Eagles have done well in recen
years, while most European populations of this rare bir
have declined. Chicks from successful Norwegian nests
were taken and released in Scotland as part of a
reintroduction programme, Scottish White-tailed Eagle
having long ago been persecuted to extinction. The
project has worked, although numbers increase slowly.

Elsewhere, White-tailed Eagles are scarce: they requi
coastal cliffs and bays or large, undisturbed marshes, a
found in Poland and the Danube Delta, but such wetla
habitats are few in modern Europe.

This is a massive eagle, without the poise and elegance
of a Golden Eagle, but impressive nonetheless, with its v
broad wings (held flatter than a Golden Eagle's), a bulky,
protruding head and a short tail. Immature birds are
brown, then streaked, with a dark tail at first, but adults
have pure white tails and, as they get older, increasingly
pale heads. Their big yellow bills and bare shanks separa
them from Golden and Spotted Eagles, too.

They tend to be sluggish birds, sitting around for lo
periods, but are also famous for display flights in whic
a pair grasp each other's feet and spin around like a
double wheel, falling towards the ground. They also
snatch fish, allowing photographers, throwing out fish
bait from a boat, to get some great shots.

Mostly N and
central Europe.

Immature

Old bird –
can have
pale head

cm. 3-7 kg.
o see Golden Eagle, Griffon Vulture, pages 134 and 118.

Griffon & Egyptian Vultures

Gyps vulvus and *Neophron percnopteru*

Many people unfamiliar with birds probably associate vultures with Africa and the tropics, but in the **Griffon Vulture**, Europe has one of the world's great vultures: a bird that provides hours of fascination as it circles overhead. Moreover, in parts of Spain, it is relatively abundant and easy to see, although in most of Europe it absent or rare. The **Egyptian Vulture**, Europe's other common vulture, is smaller, a migrant from Africa, equa widespread but fewer in number.

Some Griffons also migrate, and can be seen crossing the Straits of Gibraltar, but many remain all year. They prefer hills and mountains with easy access to open plain and, because they are such magnificent fliers, they can forage over huge areas. To stay aloft, vultures rely largel on upcurrents of warm air over hot, dry surfaces.

Only the Black Kite, perhaps, has such loathsome hab as the Egyptian Vulture, as both seem to relish rubbish and filth of every kind: yet an adult Egyptian Vulture ca also look remarkably handsome, even pristine. On the ground, true, it may be scruffy and discoloured, but in t air it becomes brilliantly white and inky black.

Egyptian Vultures often soar around gorges and cliff faces, with Griffons, or circle low over clearings on forested slopes, or above village refuse tips with the loca Ravens, Red Kites and Magpies.

Griffon Vulture

Sparrow

Mostly spring
to autumn.

Egyptian
Vulture

Griffon
Vulture

Egyptian Vulture

Sparrow

Mostly spring
to autumn.

Griffon Vulture: 100 cm. 7.5-11 kg.
Egyptian Vulture: 63 cm. 1,900-2,400 g.
Also see Golden Eagle, White Stork, pages 134 and 106.

Marsh Harrie

Circus aeruginosus

Harriers are long-tailed, long-winged birds of prey whi
frequent open countryside. The Marsh Harrier is the
biggest and heaviest. As with other harriers, the female
larger than the male, and looks almost as large and
broad-winged as a Buzzard. However, it has a longer ta
and more uniform plumage. Females and young birds
look dark chocolate brown, with variable, sharply
defined paler patches on the head and fore wing. They
lack the streaking of a Buzzard, and are more likely to
confused with a Black Kite. The male is much more
variegated, a handsome mix of bright buff, rufous-
brown, grey and black, mature adults having a lovely
band of silver-grey on each black-tipped wing.

Marsh Harriers traditionally nest in reed beds, and
hunt over adjacent farmland. As numbers increase, som
nest in smaller patches of reeds and lank grass away
from larger marshes. In autumn and winter, a Marsh
Harrier may appear over dry farmland, probably on its
way south to Southern Europe or Africa.

This is quite a powerful bird but, like other harriers,
has relatively long, slim legs, for catching prey in place
with tall, dense vegetation. It will take young ducklings
and Coots, or adults if it can catch them, as well as
voles, mice, rats frogs and small fry of all kinds.

Marsh Harrier

Sparrow

In winter, most go
South.

Male

Female

cm. 320-1,250 g.
o see Black Kite, Hen Harrier, pages 112 and 122.

Hen Harrier

Circus cyaneus

Hen Harrier

Sparrow

N and W Europe.

In summer, Hen Harriers are magical birds of moorlan
nesting in thick heather and dense rushes, bold enough
dive at the heads of intruders with loud, chattering call
of annoyance. In winter, most move to lowland heaths,
bogs and marshy ground, and they are then much mor
widespread, though never common.

All harriers are rather slim-bodied birds, with long,
slender legs, rounded, rather owl-like heads, and long
wings, typically held up in a V as the bird glides low
over open ground. The Hen Harrier can easily be
confused with the Montagu's Harrier, page 124,
especially in female and immature plumages, in which
the two species look almost the same. Montagu's tend
to breed in extensive cereal fields and on low, dry heat
and is absent from Europe between October and Marc
while the Hen Harrier is resident year-round.

A male Hen Harrier is pale grey with black wing tip
a white rump and a dark trailing edge on each wing.
Montagu's is a little darker on the fore parts, has a bla
band on the mid wing, and is streaked rufous beneath.

Females are streaked brown and buff, without black
wing tips, but have a bold white rump patch (less
extensive on Montagu's) and bands of grey-brown and
cream across the tail. Montagu's has noticeably longer
narrower, more swept-back wing tips.

Female

Male

Female

Male

cm. 300-700 g.
o see Marsh Harrier, page 120.

Montagu's Harrier

Circus pygargus

This is the smallest, most slender and elegant of the thr
common European harriers. It is a beautiful sight as it
flies steadily over rolling cornfields, dipping this way a
that, now and then dashing after a small bird or
dropping on to a vole, relying more on surprise than
speed or power. Like the other harriers, it has a
wonderful spring display, involving steep climbs and
sudden twisting dives in an ecstatic 'sky dance'. Males
also call females from the nest and pass them food, foo
to foot, in mid air.

The male looks like a Hen Harrier but is smokier,
bluer grey, with a black bar along the mid wing and fir
bars beneath wing and tail. A female Montagu's has a
stronger head pattern than the Hen, but is best
distinguished by its longer, slimmer, more tapered wing
tips in flight: it has fine lines and a lightness of touch
that is distinctive with experience.

Montagu's Harrier is a summer bird in Europe, whil
the Hen is present all year round, so there is little chan
of confusion in winter. Montagu's breeds in marshes b
mostly in farmed areas with tall, dense cereal crops: in
Britain, it rarely succeeds unless given special protectio
from farming operations. In general, Montagu's is mor
frequent in Southern Europe, especially Spain, but doe
breed north into Scandinavia.

Montagu's Harrier

Sparrow

S and Central
Europe, April to
September.

Male

Female

cm. 280-600 g.
᠈ see Marsh Harrier, page 120.

Goshawk

Accipiter gentilis

This is a woodland predator with a fearsome reputation. Yet, it merely does what it has evolved to do, on a large scale than the Kestrel, or Sparrowhawk, or the Blackbird hunting for worms. It eats birds and small mammals such as squirrels, and can cause havoc among localized species that are conspicuous but few in number, such as the Black Grouse. Where there is an abundance of Woodpigeons – and where is there not? – Goshawks can live in relative harmony with everything else.

A female Sparrowhawk is often mistaken for a male Goshawk: both hawks show a marked difference in size between the smaller male and larger female, and the m Goshawk is not so much bigger than a large Sparrowhawk. It is, however, more thickset, heavier and more powerful, with much thicker legs and a bolder he pattern. A female, when first seen, is a shock, not far short of a Buzzard in size. Compared with a Sparrowhawk, it has a larger, more protruding head in flight, longer wings with a more S-shaped trailing edge and a broader, rounder tail. While the flap-flap-glide flight action is similar, the female Goshawk can hardly taken for the smaller bird: the male, however, may need to be checked against a nearby crow or other bird, to b sure of its size.

Goshawk (female)

Goshawk (male)

Sparrow

All year, most of Europe, but rare in many areas..

Adult

Juvenile

61 cm. 500-1,350 g.
see Sparrowhawk, page 128.

Sparrowhawk
Accipiter nisus

In the 1960s, after pesticides had wrought havoc on small birds and the predators that ate them, Sparrowhawks became remarkably rare. Now, after a strong recovery, they are common and often seen, even gardens, although lately a fall in small bird numbers ha been reflected once more by a drop in Sparrowhawk populations in some areas.

It is the typical garden predator, snatching a tit, fin or Collared Dove from the vicinity of the bird table or feeder: a bird table is a takeaway shop for this predato Beyond the garden, it is a bird of woodland and woodland edge, hunting along hedgerows and bursting into clearings, hoping to take small birds by surprise. I also hunts over open moors and marshes in winter, keeping low, dipping into winding creeks and hollows. At other times it can be a patient hunter, sitting in a hedge or bush, waiting for prey to come close.

Males are tiny, bluish above, barred pink or orange beneath, with rusty faces (no dark moustache like a falcon), yellow eyes and spindly yellow legs. Females a much bigger, browner, barred dark on a dull white ground underneath. Both have broad-tipped wings and long, slender, square tails and fly with several snappy wing beats between short glides. In spring they soar, at great height, over the nesting wood.

Sparrowhawk

Sparrow

Not high moors and mountains.

e

Female

37 cm. 100-335 g.
see Kestrel, page 138.

Buzzard

Buteo buteo

If you live in lowland Britain, you may not have eagles t enjoy, but there should be Buzzards: and, while lacking outright size, power and charisma of an eagle, a Buzzare more than enough for everyday enjoyment.

Many species of buzzards the world over are stocky-headed, broad-winged, heavy-bodied, round-tailed birds prey, bigger than falcons, smaller than most eagles. They kill little much bigger than a large rabbit or a young mountain hare, and may spend hours searching for worn and beetles on foot. Nevertheless, they are beautiful bird wonderfully able to exploit light air currents.

The Common Buzzard is frequent where woodland, moors and mixed farmland make a rich patchwork – an where it is not persecuted out of existence. This used to the case in much of Britain, but as a result of protection has made a remarkable recovery.

Buzzards typically have streaked brown plumage with barred wings and a dark 'wrist' patch; their tails are evenly barred. When perched, they look thickset and upright, with a dark breast above a creamy U-shaped band. However, individual patterns vary greatly and ma northern birds are very pale. They glide with wings raise characteristically in a shallow V; they hover, too, like a big, heavy Kestrel. Unlike eagles, they frequently call wi loud, challenging *pee-ooww* notes.

Buzzard

Sparrow

Not populated lowlands. Low Countries in winter.

al under
pattern

Northern
Buzzard

m. 450-1,350 g.
see Golden Eagle, Marsh Harrier, page 134 and 120.

Rough-legged Buzzard

Buteo lagopus

A bird of the tundra and high plateaux of the far nort
nesting on remote cliffs, the Rough-legged Buzzard is
familiar to many people and birdwatchers over much
Europe rate it as a very good find indeed. Small numb
move south to the vicinity of the Low Countries in
winter and sometimes, when the lemmings are few, m
more than usual head south and west and a few reach
Britain. Here it ranks as a rare bird even in its most
likely location, the east coast, and a seriously exceptio
find anywhere else.

Rough-legged Buzzards are big, impressive birds bu
not always easy to tell from Common Buzzards witho
care and attention to detail. Look for the Rough-legge
more supple wing action, a paler head, and especially
blacker belly patch. Adding to a generally more black
and-buff or black-and-white effect, the under wings a
more contrasted, usually with blacker wrist patches.
tail varies according to age and sex, but typically look
largely white at the base and black, or barred with
several black bands, at the tip.

A Common Buzzard will often hover, but the Roug
legged is a more adept at it, a persistent performer. Th
hovering habit – fixed in one spot like a massive Kestr
is often a clue worth following up. Its 'rough', feathere
shanks, however, are of no real value in identification.

Rough-legged Buzzard

Sparrow

Scandinavia. Some
move S for winter.

cm. 500-1,400 g.
see Golden Eagle, Marsh Harrier, pages 134 and 120.

Golden Eagle

Aquila chrysaetos

Eagle literature is littered with overworked adjectives – typically 'majestic', 'magnificent' or 'regal' – because th describe this bird so well. It has charisma: close up it is wonderful and, at a distance, its long, slow, stable circling high above a peak makes it look a cut above th Buzzard, page 130.

Buzzards sit on fence posts and telegraph poles, but Golden Eagles are usually much harder to see: to find one is an achievement. They keep well away from people, preferring mountain slopes, with moorland or some forest, coastal crags and high, stony peaks. The best way to spot one is to sit somewhere with an extensive view over such terrain and scan the skylines soaring 'dots'. To get close requires luck and persistenc

People are inclined to think they might have seen a Golden Eagle when in fact they've seen a Buzzard, whi is the commoner soaring bird of prey. An adult Golder Eagle is much bigger, and plainer, although its dark brown feathers bleach to blond with age. The Golden Eagle has a 'golden mane' on its neck, a more protrud head than a Buzzard, a longer tail and even longer wir with a more pronounced bulging S-shape to the trailin edge. Young Golden Eagles have white patches in the wing and a white tail base. Eagles eat much carrion or dead meat, such as sheep and deer on the hills in wint

Golden Eagle

Sparrow

All year.

Adult

Juvenile

cm. 2.8-6.8 kg.
see Buzzard, page 130.

Osprey
Pandion haliaetus

Ospreys are remarkably widespread worldwide and, in places such as Florida and Australia, they nest on man-made structures close to roads and urban areas. In Europe, they are rarely so bold and trusting, but in places are relatively easy to see.

In 19thC Britain, they were systematically destroyed by the early 20th Century, none remained. Sporadic nesting attempts continued, but it was not until the 1950s that Ospreys began to breed in Scotland more consistently: since then, protection and publicity have helped a large population to become established there. This was possible because Ospreys are migrants, so the chances of a pair or two of Scandinavian Ospreys find a suitable nest site in Scotland, while passing through the way back from West Africa in spring, were good.

Ospreys are large, bigger than a Buzzard or kite, the size of the smaller eagles, but they have short, round heads, quite short tails, and long, relatively slim wings with a characteristic, upward kink at the angle. Head-the wings look bowed, like a big gull. From below, the look almost white, with black wing marks, but above they are plain dark brown. The head has a wide band black down to the side of the neck. Should you see on hover over open water, before plunging headlong for a fish, you'll be in no doubt what it is.

Osprey

Sparrow

Widespread on migration, spring and autumn.

57 cm. 1-2 kg.
o see Great Black-backed Gull, page 216.

Kestrel
Falco tinnunculus

Something about a Kestrel suggests it's less aggressive than what's suggested by the term 'falcon': yet it is a falcon, through and through, and can show its credentials very clearly when it wishes.

It is, however, a small falcon, and spends much of its time perched on telegraph poles or wires (all falcons sit doing nothing for hours), but it is a master of the air with the best of them, given a brisk breeze against a cli or steep scarp slope. Then it is fast and acrobatic, but i normal flight, travelling from one place to another, is quite slow and relaxed, with quickish flaps and few glides: it seems to have far less apparent energy than a Merlin, or even a Sparrowhawk.

Its chief claim to fame is its other method of hunting when not simply watching and waiting from a perch: i hovers. It can remain in one spot, as if suspended on a string, by beating its wings, spreading its tail and adjusting all its flight surfaces, with wonderful delicacy to the changing airflow. Watch carefully and you will s that, even if its body moves, its head remains stock stil making detection of a vole or mouse that much easier.

Kestrels have distinctive two-tone wings, rufous with blacker tips; males have black-tipped, grey tails.

Kestrel

Sparrow

Widespread all year.

Adult female

Adult male

Adult female

-39 cm. 120-300 g.
o see Merlin, Sparrowhawk, pages 140 and 128.

Merlin

Falco columbarius

Vying with the male Sparrowhawk for the title of smalle
bird of prey in Europe, the male Merlin makes up for it
Mistle Thrush-size with intensity of character. It is indee
a magical little falcon, found on wild moors in summer
and in wide open spaces, such as coastal marshes and
windswept fens, in winter. Some nest in old Crows' nest
in isolated trees, but many nest on the ground, typically
in tall, straggly heather. Tree nesters can be noisy and
demonstrative, but ground nesters are typically quiet an
elusive, slipping away unnoticed if disturbed.

They prefer to perch on small projections of the
ground, such as a low rock, a lump of peat, a turned u
clod of earth or a broken stump. They watch for small
birds, such as larks, pipits and finches, which they chas
in long, low, agile pursuits. They rarely use the fast sto
of a Peregrine, but have great determination and stamin
in the chase, coupled with a skua-like ability when it
comes to the final, acrobatic moments that determine t
winner or loser.

Male Merlins are blue-grey and bright buff, in good
light looking even bluer above and more rufous below,
with a black tail band. Females are earthy brown and
could be confused with Kestrels – however, they lack t
Kestrel's two-tone rufous and black upperwing.

Merlin

Sparrow

More widespread in
winter than summer.

Juvenile

Adult female

Adult male

30 cm. 125-300 g.
see Kestrel, Peregrine, pages 138 and 144.

Hobby

Sparrow

April to October.

Hobby

Falco subbuteo

Not many birds show such grace in the air as a Hobby and few use such distinct changes in pace and style. A hunting Hobby drifts and glides slowly over a wooded heath or the edge of a complex of flooded gravel pits, watching for large insects or unwary martins. To get a passing dragonfly, it might make a few quick, snappy wing beats, speed up a little, then rise to take the insect in its feet, then drop down again while it transfers it to its bill. If it sees a likely bird, though, it can put on a fantastic turn of speed, or circle to gain height and then attack in a very long, slanting, accelerating stoop.

The latter manoeuvre can make it look much like a small, slim Peregrine and, because it has something of the same plumage pattern as the bigger bird, it can be surprisingly hard to identify for sure: but the Peregrine is more muscular falcon, broader in the shoulders and especially across the base of the tail. The Hobby, a summer visitor, looks more like a big swift. Close up, the white side of the neck shows well against a black face patch, but the underside, closely streaked with black, tends to look dark and the red thighs and under tail area, so obvious in most guidebook illustrations, are hard to see.

Adult

Juvenile

Adult

35 cm. 130-340 g.
see Peregrine, page 144.

Peregrine Falcon

Falco peregrinus

Widely touted as the fastest bird in the world, the Peregrine might not be so, but in any event comes clos Its speed is greatest in the headless dive, or stoop, wit which it often attacks its prey: bigger, heavier birds su as the Golden Eagle, as well as other big falcons, must just as fast. Few of them have the precision of a Peregrine, however, and its stoop is magnificent. This not the only way it catches birds such as pigeons, ducl waders, or even large thrushes. It is equally likely to chase prey in level flight or to rise from beneath, roll over and take a bird neatly in one or both feet.

Peregrines have recovered from a worldwide population slump brought about by pesticides. They n breed in areas not so long ago thought impossible, including large buildings in city centres. They are sustained by feral pigeon populations in such areas, b elsewhere make use of a wide range of prey. In winter, they bring terror to the waders and wildfowl of estuar saltmarshes and reservoirs.

Male Peregrines are big, handsome birds, with narr pointed wings and short, square tails. Females are considerably larger, with broader, blunter wings: they have a wide variety of apparent shapes according to th angle of view and the way they fly, but a classic 'anch shape is highly characteristic.

Peregrine Falcon

Sparrow

Much of Europe, most in Britain, France and Spain.

Juvenile

Adult female

Juvenile

Adult male

50 cm. 580-1,300 g.
see Hobby, Merlin, pages 142 and 140.

Water Rail

Rallus aquaticus

Early in the morning, from deep within a dank, oozing marsh, comes a cacophony of squeals and grunts, bringing to mind a pig in distress. The Water Rails are calling. These calls, designed to help communicate with vegetation too thick for the birds to see each other, can be heard all year round, but are most intense in spring.

Should you sit and wait at the edge of the marsh, looking along a ditch or narrow channel, or at the muddy margin of a shallow pool, you might see one these birds come out into the open. They are not shy, elusive: keep still and you will get a good view.

In winter they turn up in ditches, watery places beneath willows and alders and other dark, sheltered spots, so long as they are wet. They are small, dark, rounded birds, but end-on are very narrow. This gives them ease of movement through closely growing stems. The Water Rail's long bill instantly rules out the commoner, bigger Moorhen as well as smaller, rarer crakes. On top, the Water Rail is a rich brown with lo streaks of black. On the head and breast, the feathers a smooth, slate grey, becoming more barred on the flanks. As it runs away, it usually cocks its short tail to reveal a patch of bright buff beneath.

Water Rail

Sparrow

Most of Europe,
all year.

cm. 95-160 g.
see Moorhen, page 148.

Moorhen

Gallinula chloropus

The Moorhen is both common and easily identified:
which is unfair on the Moorhen. Birdwatchers are apt
come across one, mentally exclaim 'Ah, just a Moorhe
and move on to something else. We would be better o
looking harder at these birds. There is a nervous, sprir
tension about them, typical of a small bantam. They
move in a forward crouch, pausing with one foot raise
long, thin toes curled tight before moving on with the
toes spreading into their full span, taking the bird's
weight on mud or floating weed. The books say that t
is a waterside bird and so it is, liking the water's edge
paddling in the shallows. But it also feeds frequently o
adjacent grassy pastures, running to safety, head thrust
forward, if danger threatens; and it may feed and even
nest unexpectedly high in trees.

The dull brown juvenile has a white stripe on its sid
and white under the tail – marks that are obvious on
adults, which have glossy, satin-brown and slate-grey
body plumage, and a big patch of red on the forehead.
The bill tip is buttercup yellow. The white under the t
can be fanned out surprisingly widely in the noisy and
aggressive displays, frequent in spring.

Moorhen

Sparrow

E European birds
move W in winter.

Adult

Juvenile

35 cm. 200-380 g.
) see Coot, page 150.

Coot

Fulica atra

A Coot is short-tailed, round-backed, and looks rather heavy in the water. On land it is rounder-bodied than a Moorhen (page 148), and more upright in its stance. It lacks the Moorhen's long, uptilted tail and nervy bob of the head when walking. Moorhens prefer the water's edge, while Coots venture far out on large lakes and reservoirs, typically in small groups and sometimes in large, close flocks. A marauding gull may make a flock skitter across the water and kick up a cloud of spray; and a speedboat will put the whole lot to flight, when they may well panic, looking very clumsy, possibly hitting wires or even dropping out of the air on to dry land. Coots are not at their best in flight. Yet large numbers migrate from north-eastern Europe to the milder west in winter.

Coots are black and dark grey; a white facial shield and bill make identification easy. While Moorhens have slim toes and ducks have webbed feet, Coots compromise with broadly lobed toes, like grebes, good for swimming and walking. Young Coots, with white faces and underparts, call to be fed by their parents with loud, whistling cries, distinctive sound wherever they breed on flooded pits, small lakes or reservoirs. In winter, they concentrate on larger waters, which are less likely to freeze.

Coot

Sparrow

E European birds move W in winter.

38 cm 450-850 g.
see Moorhen, page 148.

Common Crane

Sparrow

N Europe in summer.

Common Crane

Grus grus

Spring in Finland and Sweden sees the return of the Cranes, which gather in hundreds at favoured lakes before dispersing into remote breeding habitats in marshes and boggy forest clearings. Their spring display involve deep, elegant bows and leaps into the air.

In autumn, the flocks collect again and head south, France and Spain and on into North Africa. In Spain, they feed on an abundance of acorns in the open space in the traditional cork oak forests, just one of many bir threatened by the decline in the market for cork and th clearance of these ancient woodland pastures.

Cranes are huge birds, much bigger than the Grey Heron, which may be called a 'crane' in some places. They stand tall, their bodies tapering upwards into a thin, black and white neck and head, with a little red, usually hard to see, on the crown. Overall, it is a grey bird, with a tuft of curly black feathers hanging over th short tail. In flight, unlike the heron, its head is thrust forwards and the wings are held straight and flat, not bowed, giving a different, more stork-like or even vulture-like impression. Flocks create a far-carrying chorus of deep, clanging or trumpeting notes.

115-118 cm. 4,500-6,100 g.
To see Grey Heron, page 104.

Oystercatche

Haematopus ostralegus

For peace and tranquillity, there is little to beat a far
northern sea shore in mid summer, as the sun goes brie
down below the horizon, and Oystercatchers in twos a
threes and fours gather together in 'piping parties', the
heads held low, their loud, sharp, extraordinarily inten
calls ringing around the hills. Voice is a strong element
their displays and strange, ritualised social lives.

These are easy birds, strikingly black and white, wit
bright orange bills and dazzling pied patterns in flight.
They are sociable, too, and large groups at high tide
beside estuaries and salt marshes probably confuse
potential predators as they fly off in tight flocks, a
medley of black, white and orange. In places, they gath
in their thousands, sleeping away the high tide in dense
packs, until the water recedes and they can once more
spread out to feed.

In summer, they prefer low-lying beaches with shingle
dunes, rocky islets and little headlands, but many nest
inland, on grassy moors and in riverside meadows in
upland farmland. In autumn, they move to the coast, b
some still feed on fields, probing for worms. On the
beach, they dig deep for lugworms and cockles, and bre
into mussels and limpets. They are specialist shellfish
feeders: some literally hammer into the shells, others
insert their bills, cut the muscles, and open them up.

Oystercatcher

Sparrow

All year, but in summer
most seen in N UK
and Europe.

ung bird or
ter adult

cm. 450-550 g.
o see Lapwing, page 170.

Black-winged Stilt

Himantopus himantopus

This remarkable bird is a wader of salt pans, shallow coastal lagoons and marshy pools in Iberia and around the Mediterranean region, and is little more than a rare vagrant farther north. Even if you have seen them many times before, stilts come as a shock: their legs are just incredibly long. In flight, they sometimes cross their feet as if to help support the long, flimsy legs as they trail far beyond the tip of the tail.

The bill is short, fine, almost needle-like, and is used to pick floating insects and tiny crustacea from the surface: the stilt legs let the bird cover a much greater feeding areas as it wades into relatively deep water.

Nesting stilts are highly strung and likely to kick up a fuss if disturbed or should a passing harrier or Kestrel come too close. They create a chorus of loud, harsh, almost tern-like alarm calls.

Black-winged Stilts are generally easy to see on the edges of pools, their sharp black and white plumage is obvious, and they can hardly be confused with any other species. The back is tinged (variably) with dark green or black; the head can be almost white or marked with a large, dusky hood; the legs are a deep, shocking pink. Young birds have brown-edged back feathers and a white trailing edge to the wing.

Black-winged Stilt

Black-headed Gull

Mainly Mediterranean coasts.

40cm. 300-400 g.
see Avocet, page 158.

Avocet
Recurvirostra avosetta

Avocets need shallow water with an abundance of tiny
crustacean food, especially coastal lagoons of just the
right degree of salinity. In some places, though, a
surprisingly small, muddy pool will do. To get a degree
of safety from predators, most nest on small islands in
lagoon, but they are still highly vulnerable to foxes and
birds of prey.

Because of this dependence on a specialist habitat,
Avocets will never be common, but they are widespread
in scattered colonies, from a pair or two to perhaps a
hundred or so pairs. Many colonies produce few young
in most years, but now and then do well enough to
maintain their numbers over time.

After breeding, Avocets move to muddy estuaries,
sometimes in flocks of a hundred or more, where they
can still sweep their up-curved bills sideways in search
for food. You might overlook an Avocet in such a
situation, and at a distance, but otherwise it's hard to
mistake. Overall, the bird is stark, bright white, with
narrow bands of black, and black wing tips. Young bird
have browner markings and some brown across the
back. No prize for identifying it, but to see one is alwa
a treat, and to find one away from its colonies, often o
a nature reserve, makes for a memorable day.

Avocet

Black-headed Gull

All year in
Mediterranean.

cm. 250-350g.
see Black-winged Stilt, page 156.

Stone-curlew

Sparrow

April to September
in summer range.

Stone-curlew

Burhinus oedicnemus

This is a strange bird, not much known to local people even in areas where it breeds, except, perhaps, as a mysterious voice in the night. It arrives in Europe early in spring and sets up a territory on open farmland, with patches of bare stony ground, or on sandy, grassy heaths and downs. There it remains almost out of sight by day, crouched or standing still, its pale plumage giving remarkably effective camouflage. Should it fly, the long black wings with white patches become much more obvious.

In the evening, it becomes more active, walking and running about, tilting to pick up food, like a large plover. Its big eyes are well suited to the poor light of dawn and dusk.

Stone-curlews call frequently in the evening, too, making many different sounds, some musical, others not, varying from an intense *cur-leeee* (rather like a Curlew) to short, sharp *kip kip kip* notes, more like an Oystercatcher.

As farming has intensified, so the Stone-curlew has lost out and numbers are now maintained only in areas where conservationists work closely with farmers, even finding and protecting individual nests from farm operations. But ensuring that there is good habitat in the first place is essential if the bird is to thrive.

4 cm. 400 g.
also Curlew, page 190.

Little Ringed Plover

Charadrius dubius

Perhaps your best chance to see a Little Ringed Plover
to visit a large shingle bank in a Southern European
riverbed, or perhaps the edge of a saltpan or flooded
These birds have spread north in Europe with the
widespread development of gravel pits, but also nest o
bare waste ground of many kinds, from mining spoil t
sandy scrapes in industrial sites. Such places come and
and the plover population is both mobile and fluctuati
so finding them is something of a challenge, and an
achievement when you succeed.

Unlike the Ringed Plover, page 164, this is a summe
migrant to Europe, arriving in March and leaving by
September or October. It is a smaller bird, but more
helpful in identification is the longer, slimmer shape,
more tapered to the wing tips and tail, and the finer b
and legs. While the black rings are much the same on
both species, other plumage details are different, such
the Little Ringed Plover's white band across the crow
bright yellow ring around the eye; and its almost-all
black bill.

Even better, in flight the Little Ringed Plover has a
plain brown wing, a surprisingly obvious feature whe
you become used to the white stripes of Ringed Plove
And its call is a single, abrupt note; *pew* or *piw*.

Little Ringed Plover

Sparrow

Coastal, but some
inland spring and
autumn.

15 cm. 40-50 g.
see Ringed Plover, page 164.

Ringed Plover

Sparrow

March to
September.

Ringed Plover
Charadrius hiaticula

Go to an undisturbed stretch of sandy beach and you are
likely to find this bright, lively bird of the shore. In
summer, it is scattered in breeding pairs along the coast,
but from autumn to spring birds that have bred in the
north swell populations in north-western Europe, creating
large flocks on muddy estuaries. Migrants, and a few
breeding pairs, are often seen on the edges of lakes inland.

Ringed Plovers are at their best in summer, when their
black-and-white pattern is at its sharpest, and they fly
low on wavering, stiffly-outstretched wings in their
courtship flights. They always walk a few steps and stop,
walk and stop, whether to look back at an unwelcome
intruder, or to tip forward to pick food from the beach.
This is typical plover behaviour, and the Ringed Plover
a useful example from which to learn the family's ways.

When it flies, you will notice a long stripe of white
along the wing, following the neatly angled shape – wing
bars, or a lack of them, can be important in wader
identification. So, too, are calls: the Ringed Plover has a
sweet, simple, full whistle: *too-ip*. That, the wingbar and
its orange legs are enough to tell it from the scarcer Little
Ringed Plover, even with young birds, which have a dull
brown head instead of the adults' crisp black and white.

19 cm. 50-90 g.
see Little Ringed Plover, page 162.

Golden Plover

Sparrow

N and W Europe,
summer. More
widespread in winter.

Golden Plove

Pluvialis apricaria

Golden Plovers have used traditional lowland wintering
areas – old pastures or wide open spaces with cultivate
fields – for decades, probably centuries. They mix with
Lapwings, although, being more fleet in the air, quickly
separate in flight.

In spring they move north or uphill, to the heather-c
moors, high limestone grasslands or northern islands
where almost tundra-like conditions prevail. Here they
feed in lively flocks, with much fighting, on adjacent fie
until spring truly arrives and they spread out in small
clusters of pairs, each male singing in a high, territorial
flight. On the ground they call with a long, clear whistl
but can be hard to see: the colourful gold-spangled bac
and black underparts look striking on the page of a bo
but make superb camouflage on a heathery moor,
especially on recently-burned ground, which these plov
seem to appreciate.

Winter plumage lacks the black and overall looks
warm, yellowish or golden-brown. Close views reveal
however that the upper parts are tightly marked with
black and yellow. In flight, there is a whitish wing bar,
the rump is dark, unlike a Grey Plover's, and the
underwing flashes white.

Like other plovers, this species uses a very distinct w
stop-tilt feeding action, searching diligently for worms.

Vinter

Summer

29 cm. 150-250 g.
see Grey Plover, page 168.

Grey Plove

Pluvialis squatarola

In May, before the ice melts in the Grey Plover's Arctic breeding grounds, these waders are a stunning sight in breeding plumage, especially in a tight group sitting out the high tide at some safe roost beside an estuary. On to they are spangled with silvery-grey and black; a bold ba of white from the forehead broadens beside the neck. T rest of the face, neck and underparts are coal-black.

Such boldly marked birds may be seen in August, too, when they return to their wintering areas, but most are s in their greyer winter plumage, without the black below; juveniles, they are lightly washed beneath with buff.

There is a simple but sure clue to identifying a Grey Plover: if it stretches a wing or flies, revealing its 'wing pits,' they are black. A white wing bar and rump complete the in-flight livery, nicely complemented by a distinctive call, one of the joys of a windswept estuary. simple, three-note whistle, high-low-high, *see-o-ee*, car across the mudflats with a wild, plaintive resonance.

Compared with the Golden Plover, the Grey is a heavier bird, with a particularly solid-looking beak an large eye. It is also much more coastal, not resorting t inland fields except for an occasional stray, nor very often seen beside inland lakes and reservoirs.

Grey Plover

Sparrow

Coasts.

Spring

Winter

30 cm. 200-300 g
see Golden Plover, page 166.

Lapwing
Vanellus vanellus

Lapwing

Sparrow

Most of Europe in summer. Moves S and W in winter.

Whether the name Lapwing refers to the long, upswept crest in spring, or to the breadth of the wings, or to the noise it makes in flight, matters little: it fits this bird well, as do its various local names, such as Green Plover or Peewit. It is a plover in every sense, with longish legs, short bill and slim body, but it has broadly-rounded, even-fingered wings and a peculiarly rhythmic flight action, enhanced by the bold black and white appearance at a distance.

'Peewit' is simply the most typical of the Lapwing's many rather peevish calls. However, the spring song is a great performance, with throaty, almost strained variations of the call running into an ecstatic series, given in a wildly tumbling, rolling flight, rising and falling as all control has been lost, wing tips fully spread to create a tearing, throbbing accompaniment to the voice.

Lapwings have been part of the rural scene in most of northern Europe for millennia, but the birds have disappeared dramatically from vast areas as result of intensive farming. To thrive, these birds need short grass or crops, patches of open ground and shallow water. Extensive, dry, single-crop country, especially if the crop is planted in autumn and already tall and dense by spring, makes life impossible for them.

31 cm. 175-290 g.
see Oystercatcher, page 154.

Knot

Calidris canutus

In autumn and winter, on an expansive, windswept estuary, you might see a huge flock of wading birds, sweeping upwards, twisting, thinning out then closing up, now like a wisp of pale smoke, now a dense ball. These will be Knots: other waders such as Dunlins do remarkable flock performances, but none in quite the same way or in quite the same numbers as the Knot.

Knots are great globetrotters: they breed in the Arctic but can be seen right down to the southernmost tips of the major continents. In Europe, they are regular migrants in many coastal areas, scarce inland, and considerable numbers remain all winter, mostly concentrated on a few favourable estuaries. At this time they are dull, pale grey birds, with weak white wing bars and pale grey rumps, with no white. In spring, they become beautifully orange-rusty-red overall, mottled darker on the back. Young birds in autumn, like many waders, have a hint of the summer adult colour, being pale grey with a salmon-pink wash over the underside, and scaly feather edges on the back. Like other far northern breeders, too, these naïve young birds can be amazingly tame.

Strangely for a wader of this kind, the Knot is a quiet bird, with low, grunting calls, not much heard except as a low chatter from a distant flock.

Knot

Sparrow

Mostly August to April.

early
summer

Winter

cm. 150 g.
see Bar-tailed Godwit, Ruff, pages 188 and 182.

Sanderling

Calidris alba

Such a tiny bird, running about on a sandy beach, darting in and out with the foaming surf, hardly seems capable of spanning the world on migration: yet it is, by any measure, one of the world's great travellers. Breeds in the high Arctic, it spends the winter as far south as it can get, stopping short of Antarctica. Many, however, stay all winter on the coasts of Western Europe, especially on long, open, sandy strands, but also on beaches of shingle and fine, yellow gravel.

Sanderlings are a little dumpier than Dunlins, straighter-billed, always spotlessly white below. In winter they are pearl-grey above, but in spring you might find some gaining the rusty-red and black upper parts and rufous-marbled breast of their summer colours. Autumn birds include some juveniles with red on the neck and black speckles above. If pressed, they tend to run away, but when pushed harder, will fly low and fast with sharp *kwit* calls, revealing black wings with broad white stripes, more boldly marked than on other small sandpipers.

At high tide, Sanderlings gather with Dunlins, Ringed Plovers and other small waders to sleep away the time until the beaches are exposed once more. They pack tightly together, silvery and white in the sunshine, clean, distinct from their drabber, browner relatives.

Sanderling

Sparrow

August to April/May.

Winter

Immature

Adult

cm. 50-70 g.
see Dunlin, page 180.

Little Stint &
Curlew Sandpipe

Calidris minuta and *Calidris ferrugine*

These two waders breed in the Arctic and go to Africa
for the winter. In most of Europe, they are seen travell
between the two destinations in spring and autumn,
bringing romance and excitement into our lives. As the
tundra habitat is snow-covered until early summer, the
move north late in spring. They return early, on a mor
westerly route, so in areas such as Britain they are sca
in May, then more frequent from late July to October.
The adults move south in July and August, their
offspring follow later in a second wave.

   Young ones are wonderfully endearing: having never
seen people before, some are extraordinarily tame. The
wade and pick and probe just like larger waders, yet the
Little Stint is smaller than a sparrow. **Curlew Sandpiper**
are gloriously red in spring, patchy in autumn as they tu
to winter grey. Young ones are pale peach below, with
scales of grey and cream on top, cleaner than a young
Dunlin, and with longer, fine-tipped, curved bills. In flig
look for a clear white band across the top of the tail an
listen for a rippling *chirrrup*. Little Stints are smaller tha
any Dunlin, whiter beneath and straight-billed. Young
ones are blotchy rufous on top, with a prominent cream
on the back, and call short, sharp *tik* notes.

Little Stint

Sparrow

Passes through,
spring and autumn.

Little Stint

Curlew Sandpipers

enile

Adult spring   Adult summer   Adult winter

Curlew Sandpiper

Sparrow

Passes through,
spring and autumn.

Stint: 13 cm. 20-30 g.
ew Sandpiper: 14 cm. 30 g.
see Dunlin, page 180.

Purple Sandpiper

Calidris maritima

As a breeding bird, this is a rather mysterious wader of northern tundra and mountain plateaux, but from Aug to April it is more familiar on the coasts of north-weste Europe. Most waders probe into soft mud or sand, but this one is a bird of much harder, rockier coasts, where prefers weed-covered rocks right at the sea's edge. It fe on minute crustaceans and molluscs, washed by surf ar spray. Little groups of Purple Sandpipers, often mixed with Turnstones, leap aside as the waves break, or are forced to fly to the nearest safe refuge.

They are dark birds, round headed, rather like Dun in build, with a little yellow or orange at the base of t bill and pale orange, but inconspicuous, legs. A plain head, except for a whitish eye ring and chin, is a featu in winter, but autumn birds still in breeding plumage look more striped, with rufous streaks on the crown a a paler area around the eye. The upper parts have nea whitish, scaly feather edges; the under side is softly an broadly streaked with dusky grey on dull white. These colours are subdued, but the effect is neat and tidy, quietly handsome.

In flight, Purple Sandpipers can be told from Dunli by the broader band of black on the rump. Turnstone have a much more chequered appearance.

Purple Sandpiper

Sparrow

September to May.

m. 55-85 g.
see Dunlin, page 180.

Dunlin

Calidris alpina

Dunlin

Sparrow

Mostly autumn to spring.

On any wet, muddy beach from autumn to spring, the
is likely to be a scattering of small birds moving about
little runs and shuffles here and there, like so many
brown and white mice. If the sun comes out, they look
pale; if the light is poor or lines of water gleam silver-
bright, they look dark. These are Dunlins: pale grey-
brown and white, heads sunk glumly in shoulders, bill
slightly down curved and tapered to a point. They are
typical of the smaller wading birds, and worth learning
as a yardstick against which to judge the others. Dunl
may be seen in scores, hundreds or thousands, gathering
in tight flocks as the tide rises.

In spring, they are showy birds, with rufous backs a
rectangular black bellies. Many retain some of this
colour in early autumn, when buffish young birds also
look rather bright, with smudges of dark on the flank
In flight, they reveal a white stripe along each wing, a
white beside the tail, and call a thin, reedy, pea-whistl
trrrr-eeee.

In summer, Dunlins nest on northern islands and
upland moors, but most of those in Western Europe in
winter come from far away to the north and east; som
go on to western Africa for the winter. They are quite
common migrants by fresh water inland.

Winter

Summer

cm. 40-55 g.

see Sanderling, Purple Sandpiper, pages 174 and 178.

Ruff (male)

Ruff (female)

Sparrow

Breeds in NW.
Elsewhere, mostly
seen in autumn.

Ruff

Philomachus pugnax

In spring, male Ruffs are magnificent birds, but not oft
seen away from their localized breeding areas in North
and Western mainland Europe. Elsewhere, and at other
times of year, Ruffs are uncommon and somewhat
anonymous birds, males always bigger than females, bu
typically average sized, with moderately long bills and
moderately long legs. The slightly down-curved bill is a
useful clue. Most have olive- or ochre-coloured legs, bu
winter males have red legs somewhat like the browner
Redshanks. Autumn juveniles, often the most frequentl
seen in many areas, are beautifully marked above, with
dark brown feathers evenly edged with buff, and are p
dull, sandy-ochre beneath: they have a particular charn
and tidiness. In flight, a Ruff shows white sides to the
rump and a thin white line on each wing. They have a
slow, steady flight on quite broad-based wings. Curiou
for a wader, the Ruff rarely calls.

In spring, males gather on special fighting grounds
called leks (see also Black Grouse, page 68), where the
leap and spar in an attempt to attract mates. They hav
broad ruffs and curly crests of many colours: white ru
will attract females to the lek, but black ruffs get most
attention from the females. After mating, the females
hatch their eggs and care for their young with no inter
from the males.

Adult

Juvenile, autumn

Summer males

30 cm. 100-250 g.
see Redshank, page 192.

Snipe & Jack Snipe

Gallinago gallinago and
Lymnocryptes minimus

The snipes are birds of wet marshes with short but dens
vegetation and muddy patches around pools. They may
seen easily enough beside fresh water, and sometimes on
salt marshes, but **Jack Snipe** are extremely hard to see o
the ground. They feed at the edge of reedy swamps, or
more commonly in thick, wet grass, and when approach
simply squat and keep still, relying on perfect camouflag

They are beautifully marked birds, with cream stripe
above and contrasted lines on the angular head. The bi
is exceptionally long and straight. Jack Snipes are smal
than **Snipes**, with shorter bills and a dark, not cream,
central stripe on the head. Snipe leap up from under fo
and fly off in a fast, rising zig-zag with harsh, scraping
scaarp calls, while Jack Snipe may almost be trodden c
before they get up and circle low, usually silently.

Snipe perform a dramatic flight display in spring,
rising and falling overhead, each dive accompanied by
wavering, buzzing *bz-rrrrrrrr*, a mechanical sound mad
by air rushing past the stiff, widely-spread outer tail
feathers. As wet, marshy places and fields are continua
being drained, so snipe have become rare, most familia
in winter, when northerly-breeding birds move south.
Jack Snipe breed in Northern Europe and are known
only as winter birds in the south and west.

Snipe

Sparrow

Moves S and W in
winter.

Snipe

Jack Snipe

Jack Snipe

Sparrow

Moves S and W in winter.

...pe: 26 cm. 100-150 g.
...k Snipe: 18-20 cm. 50-100 g.
...see Woodcock, page 186.

Woodcock

Scolopax rusticola

Find a large wood in summer and go there at dusk. A conifer plantation, or an old oak wood, may be equal good. Wait a while, and you might hear a sharp, high *tswik*! note, or a dull, gruff, throaty double croak, lik *grrrk grrrk*. Some people hear the high note more easi others the grunt. Either way, a pigeon-sized, thick-bodied, stumpy-tailed bird, with broad-based, pointed wings and a long, straight bill angled downwards, wi fly quite fast overhead, just above the trees. A few minutes later, if you are lucky, it will come round aga performing a circuit near its breeding territory.

Its wings have a peculiar action, like a slow beat wi a quick flicker superimposed. Altogether, the flight, sh and calls make it unique: this is the Woodcock; its performance is known as roding. Studies have shown that several birds may be involved in these flights, wit rather complicated and variable patterns.

At other times, Woodcocks remain hidden by day a feed at dusk in damp ditches and patches of thick, ric leaf mould under oaks and sycamores, where worms abundant. If disturbed, they get up very fast and dart away through the trees, with a loud wing noise, looki rufous-brown. To see one well enough to appreciate t wonderfully cryptic plumage is a rare treat indeed.

Woodcock

Sparrow

All year, but many move S and W in winter.

cm. 250-350 g.
see Snipe, page 184.

Black- & Bar-tailed Godwits

Limosa limosa and *Limosa lapponica*

In a fight over a feeding territory on some winter-grey mudflat or coastal pool, it looks as if the long, slender b and lanky legs of **Black-tailed Godwits** must surely snap They whack each other with their wings, stab with their beaks and kick with a vigour that belies their appearanc of leggy fragility. At other times, they are the most elega of wading birds, equipped to feed in water up to their bellies, or to probe deeply into soft mud for worms.

In Britain they are now exceptionally rare nesting bi but numbers remain fair in The Netherlands, Poland ai one or two other European countries. They look grey a undistinguished until they flutter up, revealing bold wh wing stripes and rumps, enough to rule out the more streaked, plain-winged **Bar-tailed Godwit.**

Bar-tailed Godwits spend the winter in West Africa a migrate back to Arctic Siberia in spring. The flight is so demanding that once their fat layers are exhausted they even begin to consume their own bodily organs as 'fuel

Godwits have long bills, and probe deeply into soft mud for worms. Their bills are sensitive to touch and c detect and grasp prey deep out of sight in estuarine silt Why the Black-tailed Godwit has a straight bill, the Ba tailed a slightly upcurved one and the Curlew a strongl downcurved one, when they appear to do essentially th same job, is not clear.

Black-tailed Godwit

Sparrow

Moves S in winter.

d
inter

Bar-tailed
Godwit,
winter

Black-tailed
Godwit, summer

Bar-tailed
Godwit,
summer

Bar-tailed Godwit

Sparrow

Winter visitor to W
European coasts.

tailed Godwit: 40 cm. 200-400 g.
led Godwit: 37 cm. 250-350 g.
e Curlew, page 190.

Curlew & Whimbrel

Numenius arquata and *Numenius phaeopus*

Some species form obvious pairs, and these two are typical: both large wading birds, buff-brown with da[rk] streaks, white on the rump, and with long, down-cur[ved] beaks. The **Curlew** is larger by some way and the fem[ale] Curlew has by far the longest bill; the beak of a **Whimbrel** is more 'bent' than smoothly curved. The Whimbrel tends to look stockier, even in flight, and [is a] darker bird, but much depends on the light – out on [a] glistening wet mud flat on a grey winter day, a Curle[w] can look remarkably dark. Close up, on a Whimbrel [you] can see broad dark stripes along the top of the head, [the] best difference if you are able to discern them.

Curlews are in Britain and Europe all year round, Whimbrels migrate to Africa between October and March and are, anyway, much scarcer. Whimbrels announce their presence with their call: a fast repetit[ion] of a ringing note, like *ti-ti-ti-ti-ti-ti-ti-ti*. A Curlew m[ore] or less calls its name, *cur-lew* or *cur-lee*, as well as various yelps and hoarse notes, but it is the song tha[t is] truly magnificent. You may hear it on an estuary, eve[n in] late winter, but it is perhaps best on a remote moor, given in a special song flight. The prolonged, liquid notes, building up to a fast, ecstatic, bubbling trill, r[eally] make your hair stand on end.

Curlew

Sparrow

All year in N and W.

Curlew

Whimbrel

Whimbrel

Sparrow

Widespread on
coasts in spring
and autumn.

ew: 55 cm. 600-900 g.
nbrel: 38 cm. 350-750 g.
see Bar-tailed Godwit, page 188.

Redshank &
Spotted Redshar

Tringa erythropus and *Tringa totar*

Redshanks are the commoner and more widespread o
these two species, especially outside the breeding seas
when they are on most salt marshes and beaches. The
are easy to identify, brown birds, patterned with dark
streaks in summer, a bold white back and broad whit
bands across the rear of the wings. They have almost
hysterical, ringing calls, typically *tyeu-hu-hu*. In summ
they like wet fields, fresh and salt marshes, coastal
lagoons and riversides. Those that nest on salt marsh
suffering because these habitats are reduced by rising
levels and development, while those on wet places inl.
have declined severely because of drainage.

The **Spotted Redshank** breeds in the far north, appea
in summer as a stunning all-black bird with a long, fin
straight bill and legs that turn almost black. In spring a
late summer, these black Spotted Redhsanks can be fou
on coastal lagoons around Western Europe, but most
migrant Spotted Redshanks in the south (and occasion.
wintering ones) are strikingly pale grey and white. You
birds are barred brown. All have plain wings, a white c
patch on the back and legs that stick out markedly bey
the tail in flight. They are lively birds of shallow water.
with a distinctive, clearly enunciated *chew-it!* call.

Male Ruffs apart, the two species are the only medi
large waders with long, red legs.

Redshank

Sparrow

Widespread in
spring and autumn.

...ank

Spotted Redshank

Spotted Redshank

Sparrow

Widespread spring
and autumn, scarce
in winter.

...shank: 27 cm. 130-200 g.
...ted Redshank: 30 cm. 200-250 g.
... see Greenshank, Ruff, pages 194 and 182.

Greenshank

Sparrow

Rare in winter.
Widespread spring
and autumn.

Greenshank

Tringa nebularia

Greenshanks are smaller, more elegant than godwits, b
noticeably bigger than Redshanks and Ruffs. Scarce,
exciting birds of northern moors, rolling peat bogs an
riverside flows in summer, in autumn many appear on
migration all over Europe. They are nevertheless
relatively scarce. They do not form flocks of hundreds
like godwits, but usually groups of three or four, perh
up to a dozen, and feed more widely apart.

Finding one means going to a watery spot, sometim
in spring, but more usually from about August to
November, and looking for a long-legged, grey and wh
bird striding through the shallows. Compared with a
Spotted Redshank, the Greenshank is less likely to swi
upend or dash about, preferring more sedate progress.
looks dark backed, with a streaked, whitish head and
breast and white underside and, of course, greenish leg
Flight reveals all-dark wings and a long wedge of whit
on the back.

It is often noticed because of its calls, which ring
around an estuary or pool. They are a more even serie
of notes than the 'bouncy' calls of Redshanks, like *che
chew-chew*. With a rising tide, as the Greenshanks gat
in small groups to sleep away the period when they ar
unable to feed, such calls may dominate an estuary, ev
though the Greenshanks are so few.

Summer
adult

cm. 150-250 g.
see Redshank, Bar-tailed Godwit, pages 192 and 188.

Green Sandpiper

Sparrow

Mostly spring and
autumn.

Green & Wood Sandpipers

Tringa ochropus and *Tringa glareola*

These two are northern breeders, known in most of
Europe as migrants in spring and autumn. As with most
waders, 'autumn' begins in July: indeed, **Green
Sandpipers** may be seen in every month, moving north
very late and returning very early.

Wood Sandpipers are more abundant in the east of
Europe, and the small numbers in the west are always an
exciting find. Green Sandpipers are more widespread,
rarely seen in groups of more than five together.

Wood Sandpipers like freshwater, especially flooded
fields, shallow marshes and lagoons, where they trip
along the water's edge on long, yellow-ochre legs. A
broad pale stripe runs above the eye and the back is
brown with big creamy spots. The Green Sandpiper is
darker, with tiny pale spots, above, and the pale stripe
from the bill stops at the eye; it is a more contrasty bird
with a bright white under side, and shorter, duller legs.

If disturbed, the Wood Sandpiper flies up and away to
a height, showing a white rump, barred tail and buff
under wing and calling *chiff-chiff-chiff*. A Green Sandpiper
tends to go less far, but dashes up, twisting sharply,
showing a more black and white effect, with dark wings,
bold white rump, whiter tail with fewer, thicker bars
and, distinctively, blackish under wings. It calls a loud,
rich, slightly yodelling series of notes, *tlu-wee-twee-tu*.

d Sandpiper

Green Sandpiper

n Sandpiper: 22 cm. 70-100 g.
d Sandpiper: 20 cm. 60-80 g.
see Common Sandpiper, page 198.

Wood Sandpiper

Sparrow

Widespread April-
May and August-
September.

Common Sandpiper

Actitis hypoleucos

Although you may see a Common Sandpiper by the se
you ought to find a stony riverbank or lakeside in
summer if you want to see one well. In winter, almost
are in Africa.

It is a small, delicate wader with a tapered shape, a
straight bill and dull-coloured legs. On top it looks of
brown; underneath clean, bright white. The white ho
upwards in front of the wing, beside the subtly-streak
breast. In flight, it shows a white stripe along each wi

Despite these clues, the best way to identify a
Common Sandpiper is by its behaviour. On the groun
leans forward, runs and creeps, and bobs its head, wh
the rear body sways rhythmically up and down as if o
spring. It flies with shallow, jerky, flickering bursts, it
wings straight, stiff and unmistakably bowed.

The swinging tail-bob is characteristic of Common,
Wood and Green Sandpipers, but is much the most
marked and consistent in this, the smallest and
commonest of the trio.

In flight, too, it has a wonderful, simple, call, a
ringing, far-carrying *tswee-wee-wee*. The sound evoke
the atmosphere of a northern lake in summer twilight
a muddy reservoir edge in autumn, where Common
Sandpipers so often promise even better things when
wader migration gets under way.

Common Sandpiper

Sparrow

Mostly spring to
autumn. A few in
winter on coasts.

cm. 40-70 g.
see Green Sandpiper, Dunlin, pages 196 and 180.

Turnstone

Arenaria interpres

This small bird does just as its name suggests. In Europ
migrants to the far north do not leave until late May, a
some return in July. It is nervous but approachable on
rocky and stony beaches, where the sharp iodine scent
seaweed will lead you to it. It also forages along the
tideline on open sand. It takes small trifles – all kinds o
scraps, beach fleas, small insects, crustaceans and tiny
crabs – in a hurried dash-and-grab style.

On some tropical beaches it becomes extraordinari
tame, searching under occupied tables at beach bars an
taking food from people's fingers, extraordinary
behaviour for a shorebird that breeds in the Arctic and
migrates to the ends of the earth – the southernmost ti
of South America, Africa and Australasia. So it is one o
the world's most widely spread wading birds – a true
globetrotter. In England, where the Turnstone is shyer
than the norm, it has still gained notoriety by daily
crossing an estuary on a ferry, rather than troubling to

Mostly dark above, white below, with a dusky
breastband, in spring Turnstones develop a beautiful
tortoiseshell plumage of chestnut, black and white. The
legs are orange, the bill deep-based and narrow, like th
blade of a pocket knife. If disturbed, they make chatter
calls, like *tuk-a-tuk-a-tuk* and fly up to reveal patches o
white on the wings and back.

Turnstone

Sparrow

Breeds in Arctic. All
round coasts most
of the year.

Summer

Winter

24 cm. 80-140 g.
see Ringed Plover, page 164.

Arctic Skua

Stercorarius parasiticus

Few birds show such venom as an Arctic Skua in pursuit of its victim. It is not out for the kill: it simply tries to force a hapless tern, or Kittiwake, to cough up a fish. It is not, though, a completely free meal: indeed, the brief pursuit can be ferociously energetic.

Out over the sea, you might notice a menacing dark shape, accelerating hard, which suddenly goes into the tightest of acrobatic twists, turns and rolls in a nose-to-tail chase with a tern or gull: the contrast is dramatic. Sometimes two skuas will team up to chase another bird. As soon as a fish is dropped, the chase is over: the skua catches it before it hits the sea, then slopes off, low and relaxed, in its wonderfully elegant everyday flight.

An Arctic Skua has a perfect shape, like a gull crossed with a falcon, finished off by a central tail spike. Most are sooty brown, with a pale flash on each wing, but some are paler below and others fully white beneath, with a dusky breast band, creamy cheeks and a smart black cap: these dark, intermediate and pale forms are much less distinct in the more rufous juveniles.

They breed on remote moors and islands from northern Scotland northwards, but can be seen around most coasts in autumn, when they head for tropical seas.

Arctic Skua

Sparrow

Widespread off
coasts, April
to October.

Adult

Juvenile

48 cm. 440 g.
see Herring Gull, page 214.

Great Skua

Sparrow

Widespread off
coasts, April
to October.

Great Skua

Stercorarius skua

Skuas are aerial vagabonds, rogues and thieves for much
of their lives, but they do catch fish and other prey by
their own wits and hard work. Their reputation comes
from their skill at exploiting other sea birds: they chase
terns and Kittiwakes until they drop their fish. A Great
Skua can grab a flying Gannet by the wing and tip it
over, and is not above killing birds such as Kittiwakes
and auks: they are big, heavy, bull-necked creatures with
strong, hooked bills.

Most of the world's Great Skuas breed on the islands
of the north-east Atlantic, a large proportion in northern
Scotland. Their numbers have greatly increased over the
past century or so, but there is trouble ahead: other sea
birds are declining through a lack of food, and the skuas
have become more seriously predatory in an effort to
make good the lack of fish available by honest piracy.
How this will balance out is yet to be seen. Great Skuas
appear around most European coasts on migration,
especially in the leisurely southward retreat of autumn.
They are, like all true sea birds, only occasional inland,
generally when driven there by storms.

Great Skuas are dark brown, tending to ginger, with
paler streaks; a large white patch beyond the bend of
each wing is the easiest distinguishing feature from
young gulls, combined with the all-dark rump and tail.

m. 1,200 g.
see Herring Gull, page 214.

Mediterranean & Little Gulls

Larus melanocephalus and *Larus minu[*

Mediterranean Gull

Sparrow

Winter.

In summer, the commonest gull with a dark hood is th
Black-headed Gull. Its brown head does look more or
black, at a distance. See a **Little Gull** or **Mediterranean
Gull** alongside, and the difference between their inky-
black heads and the dark brown ones is remarkably
obvious. An adult Mediterranean in summer, with pea
upper wings fading to frosty tips, and entirely white
under wings, is perhaps the most handsome gull of all:
certainly the most striking. The Little Gull is not far
behind: its upper wing is pale grey with a broad, white
fringe, while the under wing is smoky-black, providing
twinkling contrast on a flying bird.

Mediterranean Gulls have extra refinements in their
broad white eyelids and sealing-wax red beaks. In wir
both species lose their hoods: the Mediterranean is be
picked out from Black-headeds by its white wing tips,
thicker beak and bullying behaviour. The Little Gull is
tern-like, small, elegant, dipping to the water to feed a
flies. Young Mediterraneans resemble young Commor
Gulls, but with a dark smudge through the eye – ofter
just like a pirate-patch. Their black-brown wing tips l
the white fore wing flash of a Black-headed. Young Li
Gulls are more like pint-sized young Kittiwakes, with
similar black zigzag on the wings. Neither are commo
birds, but any gull flock is worth checking, just in cas

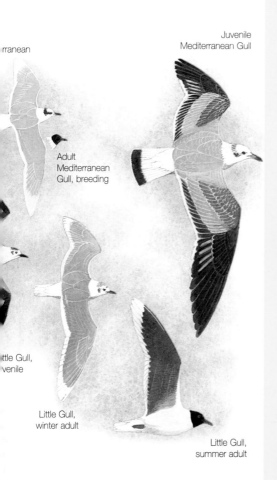

rranean

Juvenile
Mediterranean Gull

Adult
Mediterranean
Gull, breeding

ttle Gull,
venile

Little Gull,
winter adult

Little Gull,
summer adult

Little Gull

Sparrow

Winter.

Black-headed Gull

Sparrow

Widespread all year.

Black-headed Gull

Larus ridibundus

In most places this is the common small, very pale gul
is the one most familiarly seen flashing white in swirli
flocks behind a tractor and plough, or squabbling ove
scraps beside a town centre river.

In winter, it is white and silvery-grey all over except
for some black at the wing tip, a dusky underwing an
small black spots on the head – a black ear spot and
smudgy crown. In summer, the head becomes dark
chocolate brown, fading to a paler liver-brown later, b
may look almost black at a distance. The outer wing h
a long triangular flash of white at all times, contrastir
with a blackish area beneath, and this combination is
adequate for identification most of the time.

The Black-headed Gull's immaculate pattern is set c
by red legs and a red beak: in winter, they are bright,
almost scarlet, but become dark plum-red in spring,
when the birds display and fight noisily. In early Marc
their arrival at a lake, in order to nest, is marked by a
regular pre-dawn chorus of long, unmusical but pleas
enough squawling notes and fast, chattering calls: the
not as refined in voice as in appearance.

In winter, it feeds on tips, beaches, farmland and in
urban areas and gathers on reservoirs to roost each
night, often in many thousands: an impressive sight.

Winter juvenile

Winter adult

n. 250-350 g.
see Common Gull, page 210.

Common Gull

Sparrow

Widespread in
winter.

Common Gu

Larus canus

At a glance, this bird looks like a Herring Gull, with t
same grey back, black and white wing tips and otherw
white plumage. It is, however, subtly different and easi
distinguished with practice. It is neat, round-headed ar
small-billed, with a black (rather than pale) eye, all giv
a gentler expression than the Herring Gull. The grey o
the back is a little darker than most Herring Gulls', an
the black wing tips have bolder white patches. In detai
the bill is often greener, and never has a red spot, while
the legs vary from grey-green to yellowish, never pink.

Flocks march slowly across grassy pastures and
ploughed fields, or open, sandy or muddy beaches,
searching for worms. The greater contrast of the darke
back, black wing tips and the patch of white compared
with a Herring Gull is often evident.

Young birds are another matter: size, shape, neatnes
pattern and a sharp black band on an otherwise white
are the best features. In spring, they gradually fade to
buff with dark brown wing tips – a study in itself.

Common Gulls take the high-pitched squealing cries
larger gulls to a new, even higher, even more squealing
level: their calls can easily be picked out from mixed
winter flocks at rubbish tips, or on large reservoirs wh
gulls gather to roost.

Immature

Winter adult

m. 370-450 g.
see Herring Gull, page 214.

Lesser Black-backed Gull

Larus fuscus

Anyone yet needing to be convinced that gulls can be beautiful should start with this one, especially when it in breeding plumage. It is a superb bird, but Puffins a small seabirds beware: it is a fierce predator.

Its winter plumage is sullied by dull grey-brown streaks, but, once the head and breast become brilliant white in spring, the bird looks immaculate, with a fine slate-grey back, vivid yellow bill with red spot, and bri yellow legs. It manages to look a little longer and sleek than a Herring Gull, which is much paler on the back.

Breeding colonies tend to be on islands, or on flatte ground, rather than cliff ledges. On some western islands, colonies settle in huge, dense swathes of blueb and red campion, a wonderful sight. It is an even mor rapacious fish eater than the Herring Gull in summer.

In winter, Lesser Black-backs tend to move south: u the increase in refuse tips and big reservoirs in North-western Europe, this tended to be a strictly migratory species, moving as far as West Africa, but now, many remain all winter. There are three forms of Lesser Bla backed Gull in Europe: a paler one in the west; a dark one in the Low Countries and southern Scandinavia; a slimmer, blacker, more migratory one in the Baltic, perhaps a species in its own right.

Lesser Black-backed Gull

Sparrow

Mainly N and W Europe in summer.

Juvenile

Winter adult

m. 600-1,000 g.
see Herring Gull, page 214.

Herring & Yellow legged Gulls

Larus argentatus and *Larus cachinn*

Here is the bold, thieving, noisy, irascible seaside gull with a pearly-grey back, a yellow beak and pink legs: much doubt about its identity. But for scientists whose work is classifying birds into species and races, it is on of the most frustratingly hard to pin down. The rest of us can forget about the confusion between members of the species in the Middle East and Asia; and about having to classify western birds as the **Herring Gull** (p legs and a dusky head in winter) and southerly birds a the **Yellow-legged Gull** (a slightly darker back, yellow legs and whiter head in winter).

The antics of these gulls on the promenade, at the f quay, on the beach or around inland lakes and reserve where many often roost each night are always a happy distraction. Less so is the fact that they nest in increas numbers on roof tops in towns and industrial areas: th don't do significant damage, but they are very noisy, early in the morning.

Compared with a British Herring Gull, the Yellow-legged Gull of the Mediterranean has a darker grey ba a whiter head in winter, a thick, bright yellow bill and legs that vary from washed-out buff to bright custard yellow. There are differences, too, in the wing tip patt the timing of moult, migrations and so on, as well as series of immature plumages.

Herring Gull

Sparrow

Many move inland in winter.

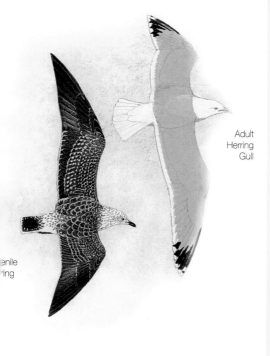

Adult
Herring
Gull

Juvenile
Herring

Yellow-legged Gull

Sparrow

Yellow-legged Gull

species 55 cm. 750-1,200 g.
see Lesser Black-backed Gull, page 212.

Some move N and
W in winter.

Great Black-backed Gull

Larus marinus

Great Black-backed Gull

Sparrow

Spreads to E Britain and Low Countries, winter.

This is the biggest gull in the world and makes no bo~~ about being top-dog, a seaside bully that likes to nest the highest prominence of an offshore stack, or a pinnacle standing above the general level of the sea cl~~ It is a predator, capable of killing a Kittiwake or a Pu~~ or, in winter, a Teal or Coot. However, most make a living scavenging for scraps and offal, on beaches or a~~ sewage outflows, just like other gulls.

It is a handsome bird, although the huge bill of an adult male spoils it for some people. It is basically bla~~ above, but fades a little to duller, brownish black in summer. Its bill is vivid yellow and shares the red spo~~ with other large gulls, its legs look almost white, or palest pink.

If you walk along the cliffs in spring, pairs of Grea~~ Black-backs – they tend to be isolated – will fly aroun~~ making deep, gruff barks: their calls resemble the Herring Gull's but have a throatier, heavier quality overall. They seem especially well matched to the windswept, salt-sprayed cliff-top environment, with b~~ sky, blue sea, pink thrift and white sea campion everywhere.

In recent decades they have become increasingly common inland outside the breeding season, feeding o~~ tips and joining mixed nigh-time roosts on reservoirs.

Juvenile

Adult

cm. 1,400-1,800 g.
see Lesser Black-backed Gull, page 212.

Kittiwake

Sparrow

Cliffs and oceans of
N and W.

Kittiwake

Rissa tridactyla

For most of the year, most Kittiwakes are far out at se
beyond the reach of land-bound observers, finding fish
bits of offal and whatever scraps they can steal from
around ships and trawlers. They live with the Fulmars
over cold, windswept, endless ocean. In winter, a few
remain in and around sheltered harbours, by fish quay
and in urbanised river mouths, not looking their best.

In spring, they return to their nesting cliffs: usually
high, sheer cliffs of rock above the sea, but sometimes
even large buildings on the shoreline. They make nests
grass and seaweed on minute projections, often close t
ledges full of Guillemots and Razorbills. Their constan
loud, nasal, wailing *kitti-wa-ake* calls make their ident
obvious. These wonderful sea bird congregations, full
noise, action and the smell of fish and droppings, are
among Europe's finest wildlife experiences.

This is a small, neat, narrow-winged gull, silver-grey
above with paler wings, each wing tipped with a sharp
triangle of black. The bill has no red spot, the legs, no
much use for walking, are short and black. In flight, t
long white head and neck and slightly notched white t
contrast with a narrow grey saddle. Young ones have
dramatic black zig-zag across the wings, and a narrow
black collar.

juvenile

Adult.
In winter,
head is grey

cm. 350-425 g.
o see Common Gull, Little Gull, pages 210 and 206.

Sandwich Tern

Sparrow

N and W coasts,
summer. More
widespread, winter.

Sandwich Tern

Sterna sandvicensis

Terns are essentially long-bodied, slim-winged, sharp-billed, smaller versions of gulls, but this one is a big bir as long-winged as one of the smaller gulls, such as the Kittiwake. Nevertheless, it still has the narrow, angular look of a typical tern in flight and, on the ground, its low-slung, horizontal stance, pointed beak and ragged, spiky crest are obvious.

It is an early arrival from West Africa, reaching Euro in March, when its full black cap stands out against the stark white of its face and under side. By June, however the forehead has begun to turn white and the crown is increasingly streaked paler as the summer progresses. T bill remains black with a light tip, which is almost colourless or pale yellow, and the legs are black: it has none of the red of a Common or Arctic Tern.

While Common Terns are pale grey beneath, Sandw Terns are unsullied white. With the paler grey upper si also obvious, it looks ghostly-pale in flight, so can be picked out with confidence at long range. Juveniles hav a black ear patch, black bill and brown marks on wing

Sandwich Terns, often calling with a loud, rasping *ke ick* note, use traditional colonies on dunes and beaches. but these are nowadays so often disturbed that they ter to move around and some big colonies eventually disappear. Only well-guarded reserves are secure.

m. 210-250 g.
see Common Tern, page 222.

Common &
Arctic Terns

Sterna hirundo and *Sterna paradisae*

The first tern is a promise of summer every bit as muc
as a Swallow. In April, **Arctic Terns** return from the
Southern Oceans and **Common Terns** from West Afric
Arctics breed on northern coasts and islands, while
Common Terns breed both on coasts and spread inlan
through Europe. In Britain, they nest beside former
gravel pits and feed over nearby rivers, so have becom
frequent even in towns and cities far inland, their shar
discordant cries turning the heads of those who
appreciate such things.

These are small terns, slender, with long, forked, wl
tails. Compared with the round-headed, short-billed
Arctic, the Common has a longer bill and neck, shorte
tail and longer, broader wings, so is subtly different ir
flight. Its wings have darker outer primaries (on an
Arctic they are all the same pearl-grey); underneath, t
wing tips have a broader, dark trailing edge (an Arctic
underwing is translucent white with a thin dark line).

The Common's bill has a black tip and its legs are a
fraction longer than on an Arctic Tern. In summer, bo
have black caps; by autumn, the Common's forehead
white (Arctics keep the black for longer). Young birds
are a little different, but on a Common Tern the wing
dark at front and rear, paler in the middle, while on a
Arctic, the wing has a broad white trailing edge.

Common Tern

Sparrow

April to October.

Arctic Tern

mon Tern

April to October.

Arctic Tern

Sparrow

mon Tern: 33 cm. 100-140 g.
Tern: 35 cm. 80-110 g.
see Sandwich Tern, page 220.

Little & Black Terns

Sterna albifrons and *Chidlonias nige*

Little Terns push their luck by breeding at the edge of surf on shingle and sandy beaches. High tide and wind blown sand can swamp their eggs and chicks at any ti Add the fact that beaches attract people, and you have the reason why Little Terns have retreated to a handfu of protected places and become scarce. They are widespread but highly localized, and most likely to be seen on spring and autumn migration along sea coasts much more rarely inland.

Black Terns breed on shallow lakes and watery marshes and are also more widely seen in spring and autumn, when small groups are frequent on lakes and reservoirs. Large flocks – even hundreds – can appear memorable days, but often move on within hours.

Little Terns are palest grey and white, always with white forehead within a black cap, and have yellow b and orange legs, with no hint of red. They hover with whirring wings and dive with an audible 'smack'. Blac Terns in spring are beautifully smoky-black and lead-grey, white only under the tail, but in autumn become paler grey, white beneath, with black hoods extending little lobes over the ears. They don't dive, but fly head to-wind and dip to the surface to feed: a flock feeding over a lake has an almost mesmeric appeal.

Little Tern

Sparrow

Spring to autumn.

Little Tern

Black Tern,
juvenile

Tern: 25 cm. 50-60 g.
Tern: 25 cm. 60-80 g.
see Sandwich Tern, Common Tern, pages 220 and 222.

Black Tern

Sparrow

Spring to autumn.

Guillemot & Razorbill

Uria aalge and *Alca torda*

These are the two commoner auks, a group of sea bir
of the north and west that includes the Puffin and Bla
Guillemot and the sadly extinct Great Auk, all master
divers in their quest for fish. The **Guillemot** is
everywhere the most abundant, lining up on long,
narrow ledges or covering the tops of offshore stacks
hordes, creating a noisy, aromatic, hugely atmospheri
colony. **Razorbills** mix with the Guillemots, tucking
themselves into deeper cavities here and there.

On land, both birds squat on weak legs, standing
upright like tiny penguins, white in front, black or, or
more southern Guillemots, brown on the head and ba
On water they swim low, heads held up, bills horizon
The Razorbill is the blackest, with a longer, pointed t
a bull neck and a deep, blade-like bill crossed by a ba
of white. The Guillemot has a square tail, a slender n
and a long, slim, pointed bill. In winter both lose the
dark throat and breast, but the black cap of the
Razorbill reaches below the eye, while the Guillemot
a narrow cap and whiter face, with a thin line of blac
isolated behind the eye.

Both birds fly low and fast, on narrow wings, lacki
manoeuvrability: they 'fly' much better under water,
using their wings for propulsion. The Razorbill routir
dives as deep as 100 metres.

Guillemot

Sparrow

Cliffs and oceans.

Guillemot

Guillemot,
winter

Razorbill

Razorbill,
winter

Razorbill

Sparrow

Coasts.

Guillemot: 41 cm. 900-1,000 g.
Razorbill: 40 cm. 550-750 g.
see Puffin, page 228.

Puffin &
Black Guillemo[t]

Fratercula arctica and *Cepphus gry[lle]*

Most people know what a **Puffin** looks like, although
detail might be difficult to describe. The real thing is a
bird of the ocean. In spring, by some near miraculous
means, Puffins from the trackless Atlantic return to the
traditional islands and coastal cliffs to breed. They nest
burrows, commandeered from rabbits or Manx
Shearwaters, or dug in soft soil on a grassy slope above
the rocks, or in deep cavities in cliffs and scree. Pairs
often return to the same burrow, but that does not
prevent a period of ritual courtship and territorial disp[lay]
Puffins are incurably nosey, into everyone else's busine[ss]
and do good deal of posturing, calling and occasional[ly]
serious fighting. Adults are easy to identify, if perhaps
smaller than expected on first acquaintance; juvenile a[nd]
winter birds have darker faces and small, dull bills.

   Black Guillemots, hardly to be confused with Puffi[n]
are not seen on high cliffs or on the grassy slopes abo[ve]
them. They prefer rocky islets and tumbled boulders a[t]
the water's edge, and swim a little way out on the sea [in]
ones and twos. The Black Guillemot is a northern
seabird and rarely ventures south. In summer it is
smokey black, except for a white wing patch and red
legs; in winter mottled white and black, with the sam[e]
white wing patch.

Puffin

Sparrow

At coastal nest
sites, summer,
otherwise at sea.

Summer

Black Guillemot

Black Guillemot

Sparrow

Puffin

N, all year.

species: 30 cm. 350-450 g.
see Razorbill, page 226.

Rock Dove

Sparrow

Coasts of far N and
W. Some inland cliffs.

Rock Dove

Columba livia

The wild Rock Dove is the ancestor of the domestic
pigeon, and it is hard to think of it as other than the
same bird as the town square pigeon, or feral pigeon.
Indeed, in most wild places now it is difficult to find a
pure Rock Dove that has not interbred with 'escapees'
returning to their ancestral cliffs. However, in the far
north and west of Europe, on coastal cliffs and islands
there are still some beautiful examples of the real thing
perfect in their blue-grey and black, with purple and
green neck patches, thick black wing bars and a square
of white on the back. In flight, they reveal white under
wings, which set them apart usefully from the soft grey
Stock Dove.

Rock Doves take off with the same clatter and flurry
town pigeons and fly into dark sea caves with a similar
free abandon, fast and acrobatic: they need to be, as they
are one of the chief targets of the Peregrine Falcon.

In towns, lowland quarries and on coasts, descendant
of domestic birds that long ago 'went bush' can be foun
in various colours, from almost black to almost white
via rusty-brown and blue grey. There is a tendency for
the old grey, black and white pattern to reassert itself
over time. Individuals vary widely: some are
unapproachable birds of the seacliff; others are beggar
seeking handouts at railway stations.

35 cm. 250-300 g.
see Stock Dove, page 232.

Stock Dove

Columba oenas

If you live close to a park with tall, old trees, or an ancient wood, or perhaps a rural farming area with tumbledown outbuildings, you may see Stock Doves every day: these are their typical nest sites. Otherwise, you might have to seek them out, and they are worth it. They also nest on cliffs and ledges in old quarries; and on high, remote cliffs up on the moors.

Outside their nesting season, for much of the year, they may be found in small groups or mixed with large flocks of Wood Pigeons out on fields, usually much the less numerous of the two. In the evening, Stock Doves, Wood Pigeons, Rooks and Jackdaws fly in from all sides in surprising numbers to roost in woods and thickets. The song may well catch your attention: a deep, rolling *coo*, *orr-woo*, *orr-woo*, unlike the familiar Wood Pigeon's. Or you might notice one in display flight, with raised, sailing over the tree tops or tacking this way and that across a quarry.

Look at the wings: there is none of the white so striking on a Wood Pigeon, but the long, central pale grey panel is surrounded by muted grey-black. On the ground, a Stock Dove reveals strong hues on its neck, bluer basic colour than a Wood Pigeon and deep, coral red legs. It is a smart bird, worth a close look.

Stock Dove

Sparrow

NE Germany birds move SW in winter.

34 cm. 300-500 g.
see Wood Pigeon, page 234.

Wood Pigeon

Sparrow

E populations move
W in winter.

Wood Pigeon
Columba palumbus

Most people tend to ignore pigeons, or even dislike the
but these birds, for all their faults as undoubted
agricultural pests, are large, handsome creatures. This
by some way the biggest of the European pigeons, and
most areas by far the most abundant. In the U.K. it ha
become one of the commonest birds.

It is thoroughly gregarious, living in flocks large and
small all year round. It breeds all year round, too, give
away by white eggshells dropped away from the nest.
Many nest in the autumn to take advantage of the
abundance of food. Like all pigeons, they feed their
squabs on pigeon milk, a secretion from the crop, until
they are old enough to find seeds themselves. Wood
Pigeons often visit bird tables, where they may be seen
a thorough nuisance or the star attraction – after all, th
is a big bird for a small bird table and the bright bill, b
white neck patches and pink breast make it a fine sight
(young birds lack the white neck patches). But it does
tend to hoover up food at an alarming rate.

If nothing else, we should welcome the Wood Pigeo
for its crooning, restful song, at its best in the last glo
of the sun on a still summer evening: a lovely, soothing
sound evocative of summer days, childhood memories
and holidays in the country.

42 cm. 400-550 g.
see Stock Dove, page 232.

Collared Dove

Sparrow

Most of Europe,
all year.

Collared Dove

Streptopelia decaocto

Birdwatchers of a certain age remember their first
Collared Dove, even travelling to see one, early in the
1960s. These days, to most people, the bird offers no
excitement at all – it's just the common dove with a
monotonous call – and you can see it anywhere. Back
then, it was a strange new visitor from the east.

Collared Doves reached much of Western Europe in
mid 1950s but remained rare for years until, eventually
the population began to take off. What sparked the
expansion from the Middle East is still mysterious.

Initially these small, delicate doves concentrated on
areas with plentiful grain, such as distilleries, dockyard
and farmsteads, but now they are far more evenly
distributed in suburban and rural areas. Experts claim
that they feed on spilt grain around chicken runs – how
many people have chicken runs? On what do they real
feed? Many fly off to the local horse paddocks, but
others visit bird tables and annoy people who bought
expensive food for pretty birds.

Apart from the thin collar and pale tip to the long t
the Collared Dove's chief features are its wheezy *kwaa*
call – it's unusual for a dove to call in flight; and the
three-note song, *cu-cooo-cu*, which, once you listen to
carefully, has far more variation than might be imagin

3 cm. 150-200 g.
see Turtle Dove, page 238.

Turtle Dove

Streptopelia turtur

Many farmland birds are declining across Europe, but
the widespread loss of the Turtle Dove is surely one of
the most regrettable: it's as gentle and inoffensive a bird
as can be imagined. The cause of its decline may in part
be due to changes within Europe, but there are problems
in its West African winter quarters too. They used to
congregate there in their millions, but climate change and
perhaps widespread use of pesticides and other abuses of
the land have seen a catastrophic decline.

Turtle Doves are the very essence of summer in
Europe: their rolling, purring coo somehow seems made
for a hot day. In the air, they look lightweight, their
quick, direct flight with frequent sideways tilts and rolls
more so than the heavier Collared Dove. As a Turtle
Dove settles, it fans out its wings and the wedge-shaped
black tail, showing a broad white band at the tip.

Whatever the problem, Turtle Doves have undoubtedly
lost ground in much of Europe as the untidy, dense
thickets and tall, old hedges that they particularly like
have been grubbed up and cleared away. They seem to
belong to an older, simpler, more enjoyable rural
landscape of times gone by. Wide open cereal fields,
motorways, service stations, retail parks and the sprawl
of housing and industry just cannot accommodate them

Turtle Dove

Sparrow

Most of Europe,
all year.

8 cm. 130-180 g.
see Collared Dove, page 236.

Cuckoo

Sparrow

April to September.

Cuckoo
Cuculus canorus

It may seem to be simply a mysterious voice, but there
a real bird there somewhere, and you will see it if you
are patient enough. You may well have seen one alrea
without realising it. It is quite a large, grey bird, like a
long-tailed pigeon, flying with a flurry of sharp wings
widely fanned, white-spotted tail and its narrow head
raised. When it alights in a tree it typically swings its
up and sideways, wing tips drooped either side, then
settles into a squat pose, or sits horizontally. It sings w
its beak firmly shut, but the soft, far-carrying *cuc-coo*
carries beautifully across the green spring countryside
is often varied with a *cuc-cuc-coo*, and strange, chuck
notes, while the female makes a short, throaty, water-
bubbling trill.

Young Cuckoos, famously reared by other birds –
from Wrens and Reed Warblers to Dunnocks and pip
have a piercing, almost irritating, sizzling note, which
seems irresistible to any bird passing by with food: th
just have to feed it. Barred brown, it resembles a haw
or a dull Kestrel, but the fanned, spotted tail, weak
yellow legs and small, curved bill help set it apart.

venile

Adult

4 cm. 100-140 g.
see Sparrowhawk, Kestrel, pages 128 and 138.

Barn Owl
Tyto alba

Most people probably see Barn Owls from a passing
a white shape in the headlights, or an owl floating ov
the roadside verge at dusk. They are, otherwise, not e
birds to spot unless you know of a nest and can sit o
on a summer evening, at a safe distance, and watch t
comings and goings of hunting parent birds. A Barn (
sighting is generally a chance event, and the exciteme
of the encounter is all the more for that.

Once seen, it is easy to identify: it can hardly be
mistaken, unless conceivably for a Tawny Owl flashi
pale in the headlight beam. A Barn Owl is pale,
yellowish-buff or a brighter, tawny-buff above, variab
mottled with pale grey and specks of white. In most (
Europe it is a very white bird, as the whole face and
underside, and under wings, are white, but a race in t
north and east is dark-breasted.

Barn Owls are famous for their screech, but it is no
often heard and is not so much a blood-curdling wail
a strangled, hissing squeal. More likely, you will hear
young birds in the nest, snoring, hissing and grunting
each other before they are old enough to fly.

Barn Owl

Sparrow

Most of Europe,
all year.

m. 250-350 g.
see Tawny Owl, page 246.

Little Owl

Athene noctua

All owls have good sight and hearing, although not a
great deal better than humans'. Little Owls make the
of their senses and look hard at anything interesting o
alarming. In order to get a fix on the object, they look
it from all angles, bobbing, leaning sideways, twisting
their heads, as if incurably curious.

It is this that makes owls, especially young ones, so
cute, and the Little Owl is no exception: but it is also
fierce, and its wide, olive-yellow eyes and flat brows gi
it an aggressive frown. Its size sets it apart from most
other owls: only perhaps a Scops Owl, seen by day, mi
be taken for a Little Owl, but the broad, rounded, hea
browed face of the Little Owl is generally unmistakeab

It is often about by day, sitting on a barn roof, or o
dead branch of a tree; or on a pile of rocks above the
shore; or on an island. Little Owls like open places, as
well as parkland with old trees, or big trees along a
hedgerow in farmland. Although often seen by day in
such places, standing out in good light, they feed almo
exclusively at dusk and dawn, taking worms and beet
as well as the occasional small bird.

Little Owl

Sparrow

Most of Europe,
all year.

m. 150-200 g.
see Tawny Owl, page 246.

Tawny Owl

Sparrow

Most of Europe,
all year.

Tawny Owl

Strix aluco

Tawnies are relatively common, but by no means easy
see – a clear view is something to boast about. They a
strictly nocturnal: even in summer, they begin calling
only when the evening shade is well advanced, and the
don't move much until it is dark.

Nevertheless, most people have heard the calls and
song of a Tawny Owl, even if only on television: loud,
nasal *kee-wick*! calls and the famous breathy *hoot -
hooo! ho-u-u-u-hoo-oooooooooo*. Calls give away its
presence in a wood, or a thicket with tall trees at the
corner of a park, or in evergreen oaks and conifers
beside undisturbed gardens. As darkness falls, pairs du
and males compete, hoot against hoot. As other birds
become silent, so the owls' magic rings around the
woods and they have the stage to themselves.

Tawny Owls need large cavities as nest sites: when
trees are felled, or severely pruned, to prevent acciden
owls, among other birds, are deprived of their living
quarters. Nest boxes can help.

They are great worm- and beetle-eaters, but take m
mice, voles and rats and small or medium-sized birds.
seen clearly, the large, round head with bold, black ey
rufous or grey-brown plumage and a row of white
shoulder spots identify this bird beyond any doubt.

cm. 400-650 g.
see Long-eared Owl, page 248.

Long- & Shor eared Owls

Asio otus and *Asio flammeus*

Owls are woodland birds, aren't they? Not the **Short-ear Owl**: it is an owl of upland moors, heathery slopes and rush-filled valleys and, especially in winter, lowland floo and reedy marshes. It is almost more reminiscent of the harriers than an owl.

Hunting, for this bird, means flying low over open ground, wavering from side to side, gliding with its wing raised in a shallow V, and diving in head first to catch a vole in the grass or heath. When seen like this, it can loc remarkably pale against the dark heather, but close up, i shows a beautifully marbled pattern of dark brown, taw buff and cream. Even in flight, you can often see the bla eye sockets and piercing yellow eyes.

If all owls have an air of mystery, the **Long-eared** is th most mysterious of all: a strange, upright, tense bird if disturbed, squeezed upright against a tree trunk, or inside thicket of willows and thorn. It erects its long ear tufts to look like a broken branch. At dusk, they are raised to hel communicate with other owls. These feather tufts have nothing to do with the ears, which are hidden beneath th flat feathers of the facial disk. A relaxed bird, with the ea tufts down, looks dumpy. In spring Long-eared Owls hoc with a soft, cooing moan; more easily heard are the 'squeaky gate' calls of youngsters in summer. These secre birds are best seen in winter, when groups roost together.

Long-eared Owl

Sparrow

Mostly all year.

ed Owl

Short-eared Owl

Short-eared Owl

Sparrow

g-eared Owl: 36 cm. 300-400 g.
rt-eared Owl: 37 cm. 270-350 g.
see Tawny Owl, page 246.

More widespread
October to March
than at other times.

Eagle Owl

Sparrow

All year, but sparse.

Eagle Owl
Bubo bubo

Very early in spring, before dawn or just after dusk, th
deep boom of a singing Eagle Owl might be heard in
favoured places scattered thinly across Europe.
Otherwise, this is an elusive bird, hard to locate and
difficult to see well.

It inhabits forests with clearings, and areas of broke
countryside with a mixture of cliffs and rocks, trees ar
open ground, often in and around deep, wooded gorge
from the Mediterranean north to Scandinavia. It is a to
predator, capable of dealing with birds the size of a
Capercaillie and mammals as big as a young roe deer.
is fiercely territorial and aggressive towards other owls
and diurnal birds of prey – with Eagle Owls about, oth
raptorial birds are on their guard.

This massive owl has the classic form caricatured as
'the wise old owl' – sturdy, upright, with a large, open
face, vivid orange eyes and long, pointed 'ear tufts' tha
are often laid back rather flat, or spread sideways. In
flight it is like a heavy, big-headed Buzzard. Only the
Long-eared Owl has a similar combination of ear tufts
and orange eyes, but, even though that looks like 'a bi
bird,' it is not nearly such a giant as the real thing. An
Eagle Owl is easy to identify, given anything like a goo
view: it is just seeing one that is the problem.

m. 1.5 - 3 kg.
see Long-eared Owl, page 248.

Pygmy Ow

Glaucidium passerinum

True to it name, this is Europe's smallest owl, a tiny
creature, the size of finch yet capable of catching a G
Tit. To find one you need to go to a broad expanse o
coniferous or mixed wood, sit at the edge of a cleari
open glade at dusk, and listen. The male, often perch
on top of a tall tree, sings all year round, giving a
repeated, flute-like note, rather like that of a Bullfinc
30 to 60 or more times per minute for several minut

Without this audible clue, Pygmy Owls are difficul
find or to see at all. They are commonest in Scandina
and also found in some more southerly Alpine forest
wandering a little in winter and even coming close to
farmsteads and villages in order to hunt.

This is a round-headed, brown owl, with streaked,
whitish underparts, curved, white eyebrows above ye
eyes, and a rather long, barred tail, which is often co
or waved sideways as the bird moves about on its pe
trying to get a visual or aural fix on a small vole or b
In winter, when food may be short, but frosts help to
preserve dead meat, Pygmy Owls may store surplus
catches in tree holes or even nest boxes, returning to
them later in times of need.

Pygmy Owl

Sparrow

Mostly NE Europe;
some in Central
Europe.

8 cm. 50-80 g.
see Little Owl, page 244.

Nightjar

Caprimulgus europaeus

The Nightjar is a bird of high summer: it may not app until mid or late May, fresh in from Africa. A strange bird, not well known to many people, it is a creature the gloom after sunset, when details are hard to make out and shapes against the sky difficult to discern.

The most remarkable thing about the Nightjar is th male's song. It is a hollow, wooden, purring rattle, or trill, or churr: this can go on unchanged for a minute two. Now and then the singer turns its head and the pitch of the churr changes abruptly, but, otherwise, th prolonged purr is monotonously uniform. It lacks melody or music, but is a wonderful, exciting, mysteri sound. Mixed with it may be sharp, loud claps, made the male as he leaves his perch and smacks his wings together, and deep, peculiar, *goo-ik* calls.

At dusk when the Nightjars are out, and Venus shir brilliantly in the west, the birds swirl and twist agains the pale sky, their tails as long and broad as the wings the body slim and lightweight, giving extraordinary agility in the air. They catch moths in their open mout By day, they sit still on a branch, or in dead leaves on ground, where their fantastic camouflage renders then all but invisible.

Nightjar

Sparrow

May to August.

Male

m. 65-100 g.
see Kestrel, page 138.

Swift

Apus apus

Even the long hours of daylight in a northern summer cannot exhaust the boundless energy of the Swift. Oft their shrill, screaming calls while dashing about high overhead can still be heard at dusk and some even spe the night on the wing. However, the northern summer short and can only satisfy the Swift's appetite for aeri insects between May and August. Among summer visitors from Africa, this is a latecomer, arriving a mo later than the Swallow.

Unlike Swallows and martins, Swifts are all dark except for a pale chin. They also have longer, more slender, scythe-like wings, held stiffly in flight. Above they do not – indeed, cannot – perch. You will never s a swift on a wire. Their tiny feet have all four toes pointing forwards, giving a good grip on a vertical surface and a strong sideways grasp, two toes each si but no ability to grip a perch.

Young Swifts become dormant in poor weather, surviving days without food in a kind of semi-hibernation. Eventually they leave the nest to fly off t Africa, where they stay for two years before returning north to breed. Astonishingly, in this time, they proba never once settle on anything solid: no species is more bird of the air than the remarkable Swift.

Swift

Sparrow

Late April to August.

7 cm. 35-45 g.
see Alpine Swift, page 258.

Alpine Swif

Apus melba

All swifts have slender, stiff wings, cigar-shaped bodies tiny bills and wide mouths, minute legs and short tails They are much stiffer than Swallows or martins. The Alpine is a classic swift, but double the usual size, a bi bird, sometimes momentarily like a Hobby.

Overhead, it shows a white body. The white throat above a narrow dark breast band is much harder to se Above, it is mid brown, not nearly so dark as a Swift. magnificent flier, powerful and fast, it is often seen hig over cliffs and mountain peaks, a bird fit for the great mountain ranges of Europe. At times, too, it flies low over broad, shallow rivers, sweeping around with Cra and House Martins, dwarfing and outpacing them. Th are many Mediterranean towns where Alpine Swifts fl low over the roof tops with Swifts and Pallid Swifts.

In summer, around its colonies, it makes a loud, fast, rattling trill or chatter. Otherwise, it is a quiet bird. It n in holes in cliffs and buildings, and, like other swifts, d not come to the ground or perch in the open. No swift are ever seen on wires with the Swallows. It eats insects caught in flight in its wide gape. The bill is tiny.

Alpine Swift

Sparrow

Southern Europe,
April to September.

n. 60-80 g.
see Swift, page 256.

Kingfisher

Alcedo atthis

Plop! A Kingfisher is often first discovered by hearing belly-flop into the water, to grasp a fish (never to stab in its long bill. It usually brings the fish to a perch to whack it hard until its muscular, wriggling struggles a subdued, and it can be swallowed head-first.

Kingfishers usually fish from a low perch, but also, especially on bare stretches of river, hover, like tiny, colourful terns. They like clean rivers, canals and poo but also fish in the sea from rocks or muddy creek sie They call as they fly low over the water, the other ust clue to their whereabouts: a sharp, thin *keee* or *ch'ke*

Why should a quiet splash or a whistled call most often attract attention to a Kingfisher, when it is so brightly coloured? For one thing, Kingfishers, being about starling-sized, are smaller than many people expect. Secondly, their colours, bright as they can be, merge beautifully with riverside vegetation, rippling reflections, highlights and shadows.

They are not so easy to see as might be imagined: now and then, in a memorable moment, you may get stunning close-up view, and see the electric blue, brill turquoise, dusty orange and white to full advantage: you will agree that the Kingfisher is one of Europe's most vividly-coloured birds.

Kingfisher

Sparrow

All year, most of Europe.

n. 35-45 g.
see Bee-eater, page 262.

Bee-eater

Merops apiaster

This is one of Europe's most gorgeously, sumptuously coloured creatures. Individually, its colours are not br or iridescent – the turquoise blue underside, for exam is rather dull. But in combination, the rich chestnut, gold, yellow, black and turquoise make a superb combination, far from gaudy or lacking in taste. It is refined bird, elegantly built and with colours to matc

Bee-eaters nest in small colonies in sandy banks or low, sandstone cliffs, even sometimes in flat, sandy ground, digging long, narrow tunnels with slightly fla bottomed entrance holes. Around these colonies, they perch on wires, twigs, dead trees or on the ground or cliff itself, posing and calling. They fly up to catch in – including bees – in the air, their long, tapered wings triangular and pointed, held flat and straight in long, swooping glides between bursts of quick beats. The c is a characteristic, slightly ringing, throaty *prruk prru*

Nothing else comes close to a Bee-eater in appeara so identification really is easy. The bold yellow throa edged with black, is a useful feature and rules out on two extremely rare visitors with which it might be confused. Young birds are duller and greener overall their parents, and have square tail tips, while the adu tail has a long, stiff central spike.

Bee-eater

Sparrow

April to September.

cm. 48-78 g.

o see Kingfisher, page 260.

Hoopoe

Upupa epops

Perhaps a Jay might be confused, momentarily with a Hoopoe, flying up with a flurry of black and white and dull tawny-buff. But in reality the Hoopoe is a one-off, unlike anything else. In Southern Europe, a few stay o the winter, but mostly it is a spring-to-autumn bird, w a few migrating farther north than the norm in March April or May, turning up in unexpected places outside the breeding range.

To come upon a Hoopoe in Britain is a rare treat. They used, apparently, to have a preference for vicarag lawns, but what they usually want is any patch of ope ground, close to trees, or a hedge, or an orchard, when they can potter about on the ground on their little bla legs. They probe and jab with the long, slightly curved bill, looking for worms, insects, lizards and such smal fry. In excitement, the long, fan-shaped crest is raised, sometimes even in flight. A calling Hoopoe in spring makes a quick, rather low, even-pitched *poop-oop-oop* repeated every few seconds.

The plumage is generally dull, pale orange-buff to pinkish, with boldly barred black and white wings and tail. In flight, the wing bars dazzle the eye, and the wid tipped, floppy wings have a curiously springy, erratic action, giving speed and a kind of buoyancy without agility in the air.

Hoopoe

Sparrow

Mostly spring to autumn.

m. 55-80 g.
see Jay, page 396.

Wryneck

Jynx torquilla

Wryneck

Sparrow

Spring to autumn.
On coasts when
migrating.

In much of Europe, on one warm day in spring, a hig
nasal *quee-quee-quee-quee* from some unseen source
announces the return of a Wryneck. Even so, it may
be easy to see. In Britain, the call is now rarely heard,
perhaps most likely in the pine forests of Scotland. O
a widespread nesting bird, the Wryneck is reduced to
scarce spring and autumn migrant, Scandinavian bird
their way to and from Africa. Most appear on the co
in unlikely spots for a close relative of the woodpeck
such as thickets of sea buckthorn. On the northern is
of Scotland, they appear in the bleakest of surroundir
Each year, a few turn up inland, some adding a mom
of excitement to gardens or parks, where they potter
about on the lawn or flowerbeds, searching for ants.

This is a curious bird, not quite woodpecker nor qu
a normal song bird. It has the woodpecker two-forwa
two-back toe arrangement, but its rather long, square
is held free of the ground or branch and not used as a
prop. Its plumage recalls other well-camouflaged spec
such as the Nightjar: grey-brown and golden-buff, wi
streaks, spots and bars and a long, blackish band dov
the back that highlights every twist of the body or tu
of the neck.

cm. 30-45 g.
o see Nightjar, page 254.

Grey-headed Woodpecker

Picus canus

Grey-headed Woodpecker

Sparrow

All year.

A call from a belt of river-side trees or open, moist woodland might catch your attention: perhaps it seems familiar, but somehow not quite right, so is worth following up. It is like the loud, laughing yelp of a Green Woodpecker, but it distinctively fades away and slows down, petering out to nothing, when the Green Woodpecker would have maintained its volume and momentum. It is the call of a Grey-headed Woodpecker.

Should you see it, the bird will look like a somewhat small, slim version of a Green Woodpecker, a little neckless in profile, with a rather weaker, spiky beak. In colour it is very similar, however, with the same apple-green back, pale underside and yellow rump. As the name suggests, it has a paler, grey head with much less black, a small, narrow red cap only on the adult male, and a fine 'whisker' streak from the bill, instead of the Green Woodpecker's broader moustache. Like all the woodpeckers, it has a long, turned-back outer toe, giving a secure grip on a round branch.

This woodpecker is widespread, but generally not very common, from Scandinavia south to central France, and into Eastern Europe, but absent from South-western Europe and from Britain. It is a little less specialized than the Green Woodpecker, adding seeds and various insects to the predominant diet of ants.

Adult male

Adult male

Juvenile

Adult female

cm. 150 g.
see Green Woodpecker, page 270.

Green Woodpecker

Picus viridis

There is something faintly prehistoric about woodpeckers, almost eerie. It has to do with their star eyes, long dagger bills, flicking tongues and sharp-clawed, coarsely-scaled feet. The Green Woodpecker is typical, but nonetheless a beautiful bird, clothed in apple-green and apple-white, with a dark streak from bill (red-centred in the male) and a bold red cap. The feathers of this cap are streaked with pale grey, giving slightly silvered look from some angles, and the cap narrows at the back of the crown, to continue as a lor thin lobe of brilliant scarlet on the back of the neck.

In flight, the bird shows a greenish-yellow rump, an moves in a series of long, deep, undulating swoops, so is easy to tell from anything else of a similar size (it is little smaller than a Wood Pigeon). It eats ants on the ground, hopping in a slow, ungainly way, pitched back on its stiff tail just as it is in a tree. It prefers broad-leaved woodland, but is as often seen on a heath or meadow as in a wood.

One of the finest aspects of a Green Woodpecker is spring 'song'. Its call is loud, ringing, bright *klew klew klew* notes, and the song takes this to extremes in a longer series of laughing, yelping sounds that echo through the broad-leaved woods.

Green Woodpecker

Sparrow

Most of Europe, all year.

m. 170-200 g.
see Golden Oriole, page 390.

Black Woodpecker

Sparrow

Most of mainland
Europe, all year.

Black Woodpecker

Dryocopus martius

This is the big woodpecker of Europe, a Jackdaw-size
bird, or maybe bigger, long and tapered, with long,
broad, fingered wings. Its neck is thin, narrowly waist
beneath the strong, anvil-like head and pale, chisel bil
is otherwise all black, except for pale eyes and some r
on the head: a triangular nape patch on the female, a
cap on the male.

Black Woodpeckers can make their presence obvio
in spring, as they drum loudly with their bills, with a
brief machine-gun burst on a dead branch, and call
frequently, with loud, rolling, ringing calls. They also
make high, plaintive, simple notes from a perch, easil
heard, but hard to track down.

Their large, acorn-shaped nest holes, with a slightly
bottom edge, are also easy to see. Occupied ones ofter
have a crescent swept clear of green algae just beneath
where the bird's tail rubs as it perches in the hole.

At other times these birds, big as they are, may be
remarkably elusive and hard to find in the extensive
woods or pine, beech and oak that they prefer. They
need big trees, but in winter may wander more widel
even into parks and gardens. Like Green Woodpecker
they also often feed on the ground.

Male

n. 270-360 g.
see Jackdaw, page 404.

Great Spotted Woodpecker

Dendrocopos major

Early spring: the woods are still leafless and dark, with perhaps just a stirring of new green. Suddenly, abrupt, unexpected and strange, comes a short, sharp, deep drum roll. It is a brief burst, but vibrant and echoing – the drum of a woodpecker.

A male Great Spotted Woodpecker drums frequently in spring, hammering its bill against a resonant branch producing a sound that carries through the forest much farther than song, but with the same message: this is my territory, I am here to defend it.

This is a stout, barrel-bodied woodpecker, black and white above, deep buff or cream beneath. A long, broad oval white patch adorns each shoulder. Underneath the tail there is a diagnostic splash of vivid crimson. A male has a red patch on the back of the head. Juveniles have more extensive red caps tilted forwards. In flight, this is typically a woodpecker, bounding in deep undulations. Its call is a loud *tchick!*

The Great Spotted is a forest bird, liking both conifers and broad leaved trees well enough, but it wanders widely and explores smaller trees and hedgerows. It regularly visits gardens to take seeds and nuts from feeders, and its sudden first appearance can be a mini shock: it is such a handsome, striking bird, outdoing smaller, drabber birds.

Great Spotted Woodpecker

Sparrow

All year, widespread except Ireland.

Male

n. 75-83 g.

See Lesser Spotted Woodpecker, page 276.

Lesser Spotte Woodpecker

Dendrocopos minor

The Great Spotted Woodpecker is a big, bold bird, ea
to see, hear and identify. The Lesser Spotted is quiet a
withdrawn, usually high in the tops of trees. It is, too
bird in decline in most areas, now scarce, if not
downright rare.

This is a woodpecker the size of a Chaffinch: only
broad wings, as it flutters and swoops from twig to t
give an impression of something larger. It is black an
white, but duller, greyer or dustier looking than the
Great Spotted, its upper side narrowly barred. The b
may run together into a squarish patch of white in th
middle of the back, but there is no clear white shoule
patch as there is on the Great Spotted. Underneath, i
streaked. There is no red patch under the tail. A mal
a touch of red on the crown.

Its drumming is longer and more even than a Grea
Spotted's, but a little feeble. It has a weak *tchick* call
isn't often heard. Fortunately, more often, it gives a
longer call: high, peevish, almost whinnying notes, li
pyee-pee-pee-pee-pee-e-e. This, at least, is a givea
in spring. Otherwise, it is a bird usually overlooked:
must go out and listen, look and do your best to see
as finding one by accident would probably take year

Lesser Spotted Woodpecker

Sparrow

All year, most of
Europe.

Female

n. 20-25 g.

see Great Spotted Woodpecker, page 274.

Crested Lark

Galerida cristata

This is essentially a southern lark, with a little penetration north along the North Sea coast (but not across it to the U.K.). As our climate warms, it may expand its range.

It is a large, pale-coloured lark, often very obvious it flies about a bright green cereal field or scurries alo a roadside, like a bright, bleached, wide-winged and short-tailed Skylark. It has something of the rarer Woodlark's floppy flight action.

It lacks the Skylark's pale edge to the rear of the w a surprisingly useful feature even if it sounds a small point. The edge of the tail is sandy-buff, with no whi and the under wing looks more orange-buff, although being sure of that on a bird against a bright sunny sk can be difficult. The crest is usually obvious enough, although it can lie flat; when spread, it stands up nic like a small, pointed fan.

Likely as not, however, the Crested Lark will draw attention to itself with its call, a loud, fluty, melodiou *pee-lee-vee* or *too-loo-wee*, usually repeated every fev seconds until the bird flies away to search for food nearby. The call forms the basis of the song, too, whi is given from the ground or in a circling flight.

Crested Lark

Sparrow

All year. Scattered in France and Low Countries.

:m. 30-40 g.
see Skylark, page 282.

Woodlark

Lullula arborea

Most people have a general idea about the Skylark, even if they have not seen one, but the Woodlark is simply unknown, unheard of, by nearly everybody. It deserves greater recognition and admiration. It is a small brown bird, like so many, but as a singer it stands – or rather flies – high above the majority.

Woodlarks are restricted by their choice of habitat – warm, dry heaths, with patches of bare sand and gravel bits of heather and grassy banks. Many conifer plantations cloak lowland heaths and, when they are felled, the temporarily untidy conditions with much bare earth are often ideal for Woodlarks.

They sing from trees, or from small eminences on the ground, but at their best when in flight. Unlike the Skylark's vertical song flight, Woodlarks undulate, gradually gaining height, and then circle over a wide area, singing as they go. The song is not the fluent outpouring of a Skylark, but a series of slow, measured usually descending, phrases, each more or less a repetition of one note: *swee swee swee*; *flioo flioo flioo flioo…* It has a memorably rich, liquid, fluty quality.

The Woodlark looks neat, squat, with a long pale stripe over each eye and a white-black-white mark on edge of the wing. In flight you should notice its broad plain wings, and very short tail.

Woodlark

Sparrow

Much of Europe, all year.

m. 25-30 g.
see Skylark, Tree Pipit, pages 282 and 292.

Skylark
Alauda arvensis

Here they are, those small birds you keep seeing in the fields in winter but never can be sure what they are: they creep about unseen, then fly off in a loose group to the far edge of the field, to disappear again against the brown earth. Try harder, and you might see white sides to the tail, and a pale edge on each angular wing: Skylarks.

In spring, the flocks break up and the small, brown ground birds declare their identity in a unique, unmistakable way as the males soar up, each over its nesting territory, rising ever higher as if drawn up on a string, singing all the way. The Skylark deserves a top ranking in Europe's song birds, with its non-stop outpouring of individually beautiful notes: at a distance only high, silvery, rippling notes are heard, but close up there are deep throaty warbles and rattles and chirps. It is the many minutes of unbroken sound that make it so especially marvellous on a warm sunny day.

Skylarks need short vegetation to nest and walk about in, and don't fare well in autumn-sown crops that have grown tall and dense by spring. Like many birds faced with modern intensive farming, they are declining, but the loss of the Skylark is a particular sadness.

Skylark

Sparrow

Throughout Europe.

m. 30-50 g.
see Meadow Pipit, Corn Bunting, pages 292 and 454.

Sand Martin

Sparrow

March to
September.

Sand Marti

Riparia riparia

Even compared with the small, stumpy form of the Hou
Martin, the Sand Martin is small and slight, easily the
smallest of the swallows and martins. For people who |
in towns and suburbs, the Sand Martin is the least fam
of the group, a country bird through and through.

It is a very early migrant, reaching north-western
Europe in early March, feeding over open water wher
insects are most likely to be found. Soon, it must find
firm, vertical bank of sand or soft sandstone, into whi
it can tunnel a long nest hole. Such places being few a
far between, Sand Martins tend to concentrate into
colonies: sometimes a handful of pairs in a roadside
cutting or river bank, and sometimes hundreds peppe
the open face of a sand quarry. These sites tend to be
temporary and so colonies are apt to be short-lived.

Sand Martins, despite their long migrations to Afri
look quite weak and fluttery on the wing, their flight
action a fast, backward flick of the narrow wings. Als
unlike the Swallow, they are pale brown on top, with
a hint of blue. While the Swallow has a lilting, lisping
call and the House Martin a sharp chirrup, the Sand
Martin makes a lighter, more formless twitter.

cm. 12-18 g.
see House Martin, page 290.

Crag Martin
Ptyonoprogne rupestris

Swallows and martins are good fliers, aerial birds for much of their lives, but neither is up to the Crag Martin. It looks chunky, heavy and broad-winged compared with the lightweight, flittery Sand Martin (which it hardly resembles, except that it is brown), but it combines a solidity and power (for such a small bird) with grace and poise in the air.

Crag Martins like deep gorges between cliffs and mountain slopes, or river valleys where they spill out of the hills on to broader lowlands, and even lower-lying places with cliffs, bridges and big buildings. They may be seen in the company of Alpine Choughs and Griffon Vultures. In Europe they are confined to the southern and middle zones, being exceptionally rare stragglers farther north.

As they fly to and fro in long, sweeping, swing-boat arcs across a cliff face, they look brown, paler beneath, and at each turn fan their square tails to reveal a line of pale spots: a unique identification mark. Fresh feathers look pale and grey, but they get darker and browner as the initial bloom wears away. These are birds without strong pattern, and certainly no bright colours, but their neatness of form and mastery of flight, often in the most dramatic of settings, make them worth a closer look and more attention than they usually get.

Crag Martin

Sparrow

In summer,
N to Alps.

m. 18-20 g.
see Sand Martin, page 284.

Swallow

Hirundo rustica

However many Swallows make a summer, it is proba
fewer now than it used to be in much of Europe.
Swallows need an abundance of flying insects – they
always catch their prey on the wing – preferably big,
juicy dung flies, or similar prey found around horses
cattle and close to hedgerows. Insecticides and tidy
farming have done for the insects, and insect-eating b
have suffered. But the Swallow remains a symbol of
summer and pairs return to the very same barn, outh
or car port to breed every year, between long, tiring a
perilous journeys to Africa. They have an advantage
most songbird migrants: they can feed as they go, tak
insects in their lovely low, fluent, swooping flight.

Swallows do not have the House Martin's white ru
nor the scythe-wings and black underparts of a Swift,
and tend to use lower air space than either, swerving
between cattle, or across the village green, or over a
reed-fringed lake. They are much less urban birds tha
the others, and a quiet, lazy village suits them to
perfection. Males, with noticeably longer tails than
females, typically pause on an overhead wire or aeria
sing on and off all summer, with slurred, liquid warb
and a little, hard, wooden trill.

Swallow

Sparrow

April to October.

9 cm. 16-25 g.
see House Martin, page 290.

House Marti

Delichon urbica

Many people confuse Swifts, martins and Swallows a
their lives, however many times they are told the
difference: but it matters little. House Martins, if you
wish to know, are the ones that build mud pie nests
under the eaves of country and suburban houses, ofte
little rows, so long as they can get the mud: dry summ
are not good for them. In most of Europe they are
frequent and in the south can still be abundant, despi
the heat and dryness. Millions of them empty out of
Europe and head south for Africa each autumn. Ther
they live surprisingly mysterious lives, keeping very h
in the air, and where most of them go is still a myster

Swallows are steely-blue on top and have dark chi
swifts are dark all over. So the House Martin, entirel
white from chin to tail underneath and uniquely mar
with a bold band of white across the rear body, shou
be easy to tell. They have broader, more triangular w
than the others, and a more fluttery flight, and tend
stay higher than the swallow, if not reaching the
elevations commonly inhabited by the Swift. Above t
top height is about right for the House Martin; close
the ground suits the swallow.

House Martin

Sparrow

March to October.

n. 15-20 g.
ee Swallow, page 288.

Tree & Meadow Pipi

Anthus trivialis and *Anthus prater*

Tree Pipits perch freely in trees and walk along bran
in a way that few other birds can manage. They sing
from trees, too, starting and finishing the long, parac
or shuttlecock fall on a tree-top perch. Song is this b
best feature, richer than a **Meadow Pipit**'s, finishing
drawn-out *swee-swee-sweee-a* sounds. Usually this is
best clue to a Tree Pipit. They like woodland edges, a
young conifers or clearings in older plantations, so co
and go over the years as trees mature or are felled.
Young plantations quickly become too tall, dense an
dark and after a few years, the Tree Pipits disappear.

Unlike the Meadow Pipit, the Tree is a summer mi
from Africa, so at least from October to March there
no room for confusion. Visually, however, the two ar
alike: the Tree Pipit looks slightly more confident tha
Meadow, and a little stouter about the body and bill.
Usually, while the Meadow has long streaks all along
flanks, the Tree has streaks more confined to the brea
with a just a line or two on the clearer, yellow-buff, f
If you get close enough to one perched on a twig aga
the sky, you may see that the hind claw is shorter on
Tree than the long spike of a Meadow.

Tree Pipit

Sparrow

All year in W.

Meadow Pipit

Tree Pipit

Meadow Pipit

Sparrow

Tree Pipit

April to October.

Pipit: 15 cm. 20-25 g.
low Pipit: 15 cm. 18-22 g.
see Rock Pipit, Skylark, pages 294 and 282.

Rock &
Water Pipits

Anthus petrosus and *Anthus spinole*

There is a limited area, along the hard, rocky coastlin
of north-western Europe, where this small, streaked,
grey-brown bird breeds: but in winter the **Rock Pipit**
disperses a little more widely, on to low-lying beache
with piers and groynes, or into saltmarsh creeks.

It is unmistakably a pipit in its slender form, with a
longish tail, standing taller on longer legs than a lark
with a thinner bill. Compared with the other pipits, it
looks duller, greyer, or more olive-brown, a little yello
below, with wider, softer streaks. The pale grey, rathe
than white, outer tail feathers are rarely of much valu
but the fact that the legs look dark, blackish or reddis
brown, rather than pink, is a more reliable feature.

Meadow Pipits (page 292) make high, thin *seeep*
notes: Rock Pipits have a slightly thicker, huskier *swe*
The song is remarkably similar in pattern, and in the
manner of delivery in a song flight that rises from th
ground and parachutes back on outstretched wings.

In winter, Rock Pipits need to be distinguished fro
closely similar **Water Pipits**, relatives from the mount
ranges of middle Europe that move to low-lying coas
and marshes. The differences are subtle, but the Wate
Pipit has a whiter under side and clearer, dull white v
bars, and it tends to be much less approachable.

Rock Pipit

Sparrow

N and W coasts of
Europe.

Rock Pipit

Water Pipit

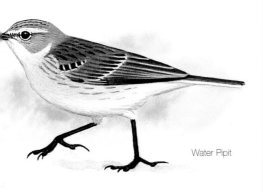

Water Pipit

Sparrow

Summer, in Alps,
winter, moves down
to coastal areas.

Pipit: 17 cm. 22-26 g.
Pipit: 17 cm. 19-25 g.
see Meadow Pipit, page 292.

Yellow Wagta

Motacilla flava

Throughout Europe, Yellow Wagtails appear each spri
in bewildering variations: blue-headed, grey-headed,
black-headed and several local types, including the gre
and yellow-headed birds of the U.K. These last, indee
might be distinct enough to warrant a separate species
does the black-headed group of south-eastern Europe.
are otherwise much alike: greenish above, bright yello
below on males, paler, more olive and buff on females
They have long, white-sided tails, spindly black legs an
distinctive flight: a series of long, sweeping undulation
during which they give a characteristic sweep call.

They like damp ground, including grassy pastures w
horses and cattle, which attract plentiful insects, and h
become scarce in many areas as the countryside has
become drier and tidier. Cereal fields near gravel pits
often have to suffice in spring. A male in a fresh green
crop looks the brightest, yellowest bird imaginable.

In autumn, when there are many dull, buff-ish your
ones about, they get together in sizeable flocks, scatter
around the muddy shores of reservoirs. These flocks in
turn join into larger congregations to spend each nigh
deep within a large reedbed. Then they make their an
journey to Africa, where the wagtails that skittered ab
chasing insects in Europe's horse paddocks can be see
feeding at the feet of wildebeest, buffaloes and elepha

Yellow Wagtail

Sparrow

Summer.

Male,
Blue-headed

Female

m. 16-20 g.
see Grey Wagtail, page 298.

Grey Wagta
Motacilla cinerea

The eye-catching feature of a Grey Wagtail, besides it
particularly long and mobile tail, is a flash of yellow
beneath the tail. Confusingly, this yellow, seen on eve
the dullest juvenile, suggests to most people that they
have seen a Yellow Wagtail, not a Grey. Spring males
have lemon yellow from breast to tail, although all ot
plumages are much more buff below.

Whereas Yellow Wagtails are the shortest-tailed of
wagtails, this species has the longest tail. Yellow Wag
have long black legs while the Grey has short, pinkish
ones. Male Greys in summer have black chins, unlike
variety of Yellow Wagtail. Yellow Wagtails like grassy
places, whereas Greys prefer tumbling rocky streams.
And Yellow Wagtails vacate Europe in winter, wherea
Greys become more widespread, leaving the hills and
even visiting garden ponds and standing water anywh
from a gravel pit to a puddle on a flat roof.

In flight they show a broad white band along the u
wing as they dash away at the least disturbance, usual
with a sharp, metallic *chik* or *chitik*, higher pitched th
Pied Wagtail's call and usually the best clue that a Gre
Wagtail is around. In summer, this same call easily
penetrates the noise of rushing water in a mountain
stream, as does the high, silvery, needle-sharp song.

Grey Wagtail

Sparrow

All year, most of
Europe.

Winter male or female

Male, summer

19 cm. 17-23 g.
see Yellow Wagtail, Pied Wagtail, pages 296 and 300.

Pied Wagtail

Motacilla alba

'Little trotty wagtail', the English poet John Clare wrote of this bird, and it sums the creature up neatly. It is small – like a sparrow with a longer tail – and full of energy, walking, running, tripping along on open ground in search of food. It likes the edge of a stream or pool of any kind, but is happy on damp or ploughed fields, and it has become something of a specialist on tarmac. It is the bird most likely to be seen on a suburban footpath, in a car park or even the town square. There, it is so frequently disturbed that, often as not, it flies up on to the nearest roof with its characteristic *tissik* call.

From rooftops it makes a more liquid call, *shwe-ree*, or combines both of these sounds with rattles and quiet warbles in a summer song. In winter, Pied Wagtails also like towns, and urban areas or such busy places as railway stations: they flock to roost on roofs or in city centre trees in order to take advantage of the extra warmth compared with the open countryside. A bird that is usually seen in ones, twos or at most small, loose groups, can then be found in hundreds, all facing the same way, filling the trees like Christmas decorations.

In most of mainland Europe, this species is grey-backed and described as the White Wagtail. In the UK the black-backed variety is more typical, and known as the Pied Wagtail.

Pied Wagtail

Sparrow

Summer, N and E.

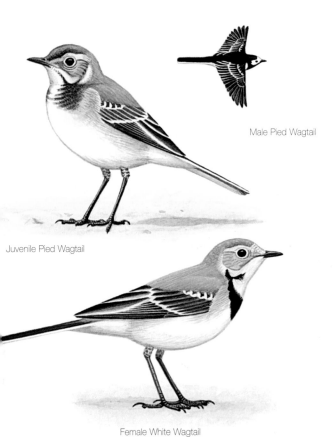

Male Pied Wagtail

Juvenile Pied Wagtail

Female White Wagtail

m. 20-25 g.
see Grey Wagtail, page 298.

Waxwing

Bombycilla garrulus

In summer, the Waxwing is a bird of far northern fore
and endless days, an insect-eater, remote and known
few. In winter, it might move around within Scandina
or, under certain circumstances, it may move southwa
and westwards right across mainland Europe as far a
Britain and Ireland.

The biggest movements are triggered by population
swelling to a critical point, after a successful run of
breeding seasons, combined with a failure of the berr
crop. The birds are forced to move in search of food,
Waxwings in winter are inveterate berry eaters: they
gorge on hawthorns, cotoneasters, rowan berries, sma
crab apples and the like, stopping at intervals to gath
in a tree top, or to drop to a puddle to drink.

They are unique in Europe, with an upstanding cre
velvety-black bib, squat body, short, yellow-tipped tai
and parrot-like feeding actions. For a bird with such
short legs, it is remarkably agile. By spring, flocks ma
wander ceaselessly, forced to eat buds and tree flower
once the berries are gone, until they can move north
again and find their summer insect fare.

Waxwings have a call matched only occasionally b
Greenfinch: a fast, shrill, whistling trill, *srrrreeee*. For
most of us, who might hope to see Waxwings every fe
years at best, it is an exciting sound.

Waxwing

Sparrow

Usually scarce.

n. 60-80 g.
see Starling, page 412.

Dipper
Cinclus cinclus

Just as the Treecreeper is confined to a life on tree bar[k] so the Dipper is confined to the edge of a stream, at b[est] with a visit now and then to a lake. It must have clea[r] flowing water, with plenty of invertebrate life, such as caddis fly larvae. Pollution, especially the insidious acidification of waters surrounded by conifer plantatio[ns] has done for Dippers on many an upland stream. It prefers a tree-lined stretch, with pebbly runs and a scattering of boulders, large and small, on which it ca[n] perch. It has long, strong legs and feet to give it a stro[ng] grip on the rocks and the bottom of the stream, and it can swim, dive and walk under water with ease, using [the] smooth shape of its body to maintain downward press[ure] and keep it close to the bottom while it searches for fo[od].

The Dipper is easily recognised as a short-tailed, thrush-sized bird, almost black but for its bold white [bib.] U.K. birds have a browner head and back than main[land] European birds, which are blacker. Juveniles are grey[er] than adults.

Dippers tend to be there one moment, gone the ne[xt:] they dart away when disturbed, dashing low along th[e] line of the stream, with a series of short, metallic, *zic* notes. They sing very well, with a loud, far-carrying, varied warble that penetrates the sound of rushing wa[ter.]

Dipper

Sparrow

All year.

n. 60-70 g.

Wren
Troglodytes troglodytes

With so little weight inside that minute, if portly, fra▮
the Wren can use its strong toes to get a firm grip
wherever it goes, to explore the darkest, deepest, mo▮
cobwebby places behind the garden shed, under the
overhanging roots of a roadside ditch, in the shade o▮
blackberry thicket or in any kind of tangle inside a w▮
or hedge. It spends much of its time undercover, now▮
then surfacing, as if dazzled by the light, bobbing and
flicking, tail cocked, and giving a series of irritable,
scolding calls. Then it buzzes on for a few yards to d▮
into a new jungle.

Now and then a Wren might be seen high in a tree▮
enjoying the airy branches closer to the sky. Its song▮
real claim to fame: remarkably bright, loud and fast,▮
more full-throated than a Dunnock's, less rambling t▮
a Robin's. In the middle a low, rapid trill removes an▮
doubt whose it is.

The male makes several rough nests in the spring,▮
which he leads the female, who, naturally, has the fir▮
choice of which shall be used, and sets about finishin▮
In winter, Wrens roost in nest boxes: on cold nights,▮
score or more might squeeze inside one box to keep
warm – little warmth and energy can be stored inside
such a tiny body.

Wren

Sparrow

Summer only in N.

cm. 8-12 g.
see Dunnock, page 308.

Dunnock

Prunella modularis

This small, sober bird is the centre of long-running controversy over its name. Known almost universally the Hedge Sparrow for decades, it then became the Dunnock, which stuck pretty well through both popu usage and references in books and bird literature. But was not enough for some reformers, who insisted it become the Hedge Accentor – or even the Dunnock Accentor – to make clear its relationship with other accentors in Europe and Asia. Now it is described as Hedge Accentor in official lists, a nod in the direction its original name, although it is clearly no sparrow. T new name has however failed to achieve popular supp and Dunnock looks like sticking at least for a while.

It's distinguished from the true sparrows by its slen bill, the deep greyness around the head and breast and streaks of brown on the flanks. A close view even reve pale eye. And it sings rather better than a sparrow, wi fast, quite bright, but rather flat little warble, not eno to match the best of the warblers.

Dunnocks shuffle along, with little two-footed hops always in a hunched, self-effacing sort of way. But the indulge in social displays, waving one or both wings. like gardens, but are equally at home in woods, on bu heaths and even the lowest wind-blown thickets on cl islands and moors.

Dunnock

Sparrow

Most of Europe,
all year.

n. 20-24 g.
see Wren, page 306.

Robin

Erithacus rubecula

Belying the corny Christmas card image or indeed its everyday status as an ultra-tame garden bird, here is a species worthy of close attention. It is a small chat, on of a group of song birds related to the thrushes.

Essentially a forest species, it is adapted to life cent around larger animals that root in soft earth, turning worms and grubs which are then easy prey for such a bold, opportunist operator. Originally, it may have followed wild pigs in the woodlands. Now it is more likely to pay close attention to a gardener.

Robins are common on bushy heaths, hiding in thickets and bushes browsed into tight shapes by pon and, in a typical Robin way, dropping down to take f from the ground.

Its perky, cocky, character, drooping its wings besid the tail, with a frequent dip of the head and flick of t wings, make it easily identifiable, even in silhouette. A the nervy *tic tic* call, and the Robin 'package' is uniqu For most of the year, Robins sing; in spring with a strong, flowing warble. After a late summer break, w the birds moult, the song is more wistful, almost sorrowful, especially on a fading mid winter afternoo Robins have responded, too, to suburban life and sin night long in the glow of our streetlights, or security lights in industrial sites or car parks.

Robin

Sparrow

All year, except in N.

Adult

Juvenile

Juvenile

m. 18-20 g.
see Redstart, page 316.

Nightingale & Thrush Nightinga

Luscinia megarhynchos and
Luscinia luscinia

Can a bird's song be so universally praised that the
reality disappoints? Well, no, the **Nightingale's** song i
never a disappointment, but it surprises people who h
it for the first time. It is well described as the
performance of a flawed genius: there is purity of not
richness of sound, variety of pitch and pace and
phrasing, but it sometimes lacks an overall structure t
hold it all together. It is often a stop-start performanc
as if the bird is not really committed.

This can be especially true of the song when heard by
day, which it often is. After dark, when other sounds ar
eliminated and the Nightingale takes centre stage, the s
can be magnificent. It is distinguished by richness and
persistence (unlike the briefer phrase of a Blackcap), an
changes in pace from slow, sweet crescendos to fast,
throaty, trills – these last, especially, rule out the Blackb

Nightingales are hard to see, and localized in their
distribution, requiring thickets that are thick down to
ground level – it does not like bushes with tall, open
stems. To find one is a matter of patience and care:
recognizing the low, grating, frog-like *kerrr* call is a h

The **Thrush Nightingale** is a rare bird of the north
east, with an equally fine song, whose duller colour a
mottled chest help identify it.

Nightingale

Sparrow

April to September.

Thrush Nightingale

Nightingale

species 16 cm. 20-25 g.
see Robin, page 310.

Thrush Nightingale

Sparrow

April to September.

Bluethroat
Luscinia svecica

Bluethroats are relatively widespread in Europe – beautif
coloured and excellent songsters, but not so well known
they might be. They are birds of dank willow thickets be
reed beds and marshes. In Britain, where they do not nes
they are unknown: only keen birdwatchers will hope to s
one, on migration in spring or autumn, almost always or
the coast or an offshore island.

This is a Robin-like bird. In spring, males have a de
gorget of exceedingly bright, pure blue, marked with a
central spot of red or white according to the local race
In autumn and winter, most of the blue has gone, leav
marks of black and rufous on the throat and chest, m
the same as the female all year. More useful, then, is t
white stripe over the eye and, if you get a glimpse, a
patch of rusty-red each side of the tail, close to the ba
rather than all the way along, as on a Redstart.

It is hard to get a close view of a migrating Bluethr
as they tend to creep about deep under cover, inside t
bushes on dunes, or beside dense stands of reed. They
have the familiar rounded, perky, tail-down, head-up
stance of a Robin, but scuttle away at speed if alarme
quickly going out of sight.

Bluethroat

Sparrow

Rare migrant in UK.

ale

ale

enile

cm. 15-23 g.
see Robin, Redstart, pages 310 and 316.

Redstart & Black Redsta

Phoenicurus phoenicurus and
Phoenicurus ochruros

There is a group of small birds, including the redstarts
the Robin and the nightingales, which falls somewhere
between the larger thrushes and the wheatears and cha
They are a little like miniature thrushes in form, stoute
than most warblers, sitting more upright on thicker leg
marked by big dark eyes in rounded heads. The **Redst**
is also strongly patterned, the spring male having a bo
white forehead against his inky-black bib and grey bac

Males, and the browner females, share a rusty-oran
rump and tail, which is constantly flickered or tremble
and catches the eye in flight. In autumn males lose the
sharpness of the spring pattern.

The **Black Redstart** is seen (in Europe) year round i
towns, and around cliffs and quarries: it is greyer than
the Redstart, with a darker rump. The Redstart is a
summer bird, which prefers old oak woods and the ed
of woods where old, gnarled trees thin out on to rocky
hillsides and moors.

The male Redstart has a sweet but brief song, starti
with several deep *srree srree srree* notes before a warb
and rattle that is over almost before it has begun. Onc
recognized, it is easily identified and often enables you
spot the bird, until then unnoticed, singing from the v
top of a tall, isolated tree.

Redstart

Sparrow

April to October.

Female Redstarts,
browner than male.

...ng male Black Redstart.
...ale similar: duller,
...er than male

Black Redstart

Sparrow

All year in S.

...start: 13 cm. 12-18 g.
...k Redstart: 14 cm. 12-18 g.
...see Robin, page 310.

Whinchat

Erithacus rubecula

Rough ground with unkempt grass, thistles, cow parsley, bracken and nettles is, these days, for ever being tidied up; which means that the Whinchat is losing its habitat and retreating to hills and moors with extensive heath and bracken. It has disappeared from huge areas of lowland Europe where obsessive tidying of the countryside has defeated it: it needs some rough, open ground with tall stems on which to perch, but that, it seems, is too much to ask.

It is a shame to lose such a lovely little bird. It sings like a Robin, with guttural churrs and rattles thrown in with the rich warbles. It is strikingly patterned, and has beautiful colouring of rich browns, cream, black, white and apricot.

Whinchats look a little like Stonechats and behave in a similar way, often perching on tops of bushes or up on telephone wires. But they always have pale throats and mostly a bolder white stripe over the eye: to be sure on difficult cases (usually autumn juveniles) look for the white patch each side of the tail. Females are paler than males and browner on the head, with a cream stripe over the eye. Whinchats are in Europe only from April to October: at other times, any small chat perched atop a slender stalk is likely to be a Stonechat.

Whinchat

Sparrow

April to September
over most of Europe.

Summer male

Spring male

n. 17-20 g.
see Stonechat, page 320.

Stonechat

Saxicola torquata

If you walk across a heath or along a coastal footpath above sloping cliffs, where there are clumps of gorse broom, or a dense growth of heather, you are likely to come across a Stonechat or two. After severe winters, when inland populations suffer in the frosts, Stonechats tend to be largely coastal birds, but in milder periods they move back into inland habitats again and become more numerous.

They tend to sit rather stolidly, quietly surveying the scene: in reality, they are looking for small insects, which they catch after a quick drop to the ground. In spring and summer, when there are small chicks about, they take on a more irascible air, and become highly strung, chat-chatting noisily at intruders, large or small. To be Stonechat at such times must be a real trial: they are forever alert and alarmed. The call gives them their name, shared with the whole family of 'chats': it is just like a couple of small stones being tapped together, with sweet, short '*wheet*' notes mixed in.

Spring males are superb in their black, white and rufous colouring, but other plumages are duller, brown often paler on the throat. Nevertheless, the contrast of dark throat against the pale breast is enough to tell the resident bird from the summer-only Whinchat.

Stonechat

Sparrow

All year in W.

Spring male

Female

n. 14-17 g.
ee Whinchat, page 318.

Wheatear

Oenanthe oenanthe

It has been said that the first Wheatear of spring will strike you as the most beautiful bird you have seen. F arrivals in March are apt to be males, handsome in th exceptionally clean, fresh-looking plumage of pale gre white, black and cream. The strength of colour on th breast varies, from clotted cream to pale peach. Larg birds, on their way from Africa to Greenland, appear May and have slightly browner backs and deeper apr undersides. The black mask is obvious, but, even on browner females, the classic Wheatear feature is reve in flight – a huge white splash on the rump and tail, a thick black T shape on the tail tip. You can be sure what you are seeing, even in a short glimpse.

Wheatears are ground birds and like to stand on o spaces such as a ploughed field or an area of short gr – a coastal golf course is ideal – and one will usually ahead of you as you go, settling just a little ahead un you catch up, then going on a little further, to look b over its shoulder. When settled, it can become all but invisible, but every short flight instantly reveals that catching white rump, which, in most of Europe, is enough to clinch the identification.

Wheatear

Sparrow

March to October.

Female

. 20-30 g.
see Stonechat, page 320.

Ring Ouze

Turdus torquatus

Ring Ouzel

Sparrow

March to
September.

Here is a bird of granite crags, gritstone tors and
tumbling screes: the kind of places often disturbed by
weekend walkers escaping to the hills. It is declining in
many areas, but the rocks remain the same and
disturbance is not always to blame: it seems that, for
its 'tough mountain Blackbird' persona, the Ring Ouzel
needs some open grass to feed on and heather in which
to nest. If these dwindle, the Ring Ouzels go, too: just
one of many effects of a warming climate. Remaining
Ring Ouzels are likely to be higher up, as low-level
territories are deserted.

To look at, this is a cross between the Mistle Thrush,
with its long wings and swift flight, and the ebony
Blackbird. However, the male has a broad white crescent
across the chest and pale feather edges give the wing a
lighter look. The brown female has a duller, but still
distinct, impression of the gorget. A Ring Ouzel is shy,
to disappear over a ridge, throwing a harsh chacking call
over its shoulder as it goes. Its song is a loud, wild,
repetitive pipe. In autumn, Ring Ouzels head for North
Africa, returning very early in spring. Migrants drop in
downland or coastal bushes for a few hours, or hang
about a hawthorn thicket full of berries, in order to re

Male

m. 100-125 g.
see Blackbird, page 326.

Blackbird

Turdus merula

Blackbird

Sparrow

In N, summer only.

Why some birds are beautifully camouflaged and oth
so strikingly obvious is not at all clear. A male Black
on a lawn is hard to miss, but his intense blackness i
its finest when contrasted with the vivid greens of a
sunlit woodland in summer. This is a handsome bird
off by a bright orange-yellow bill and a yellow eyerin
the plumage is entirely black, varying from sooty on
wings, or on old, worn, faded feathers, to shiny, alme
glossed, on the body of a male at his best.

Females, however, are dark-oak brown and give av
their true thrush natures by a varying degree of spott
or streaking on the throat: sometimes the chin is alm
dull white except for these dark streaks. Juveniles, wl
hop about giving throaty, chirruping calls, wanting tc
fed by their parents, look more ginger-brown at first.

The chief glory of a Blackbird is its song: throaty,
and melodious, often said to be the nearest to humar
music in the European bird world. Much less appeali
are the monotonously repeated alarm notes at dusk c
the presence of a cat, and the hysterical, staccato call
that greet a Magpie anywhere near a Blackbird nest.
These strident, discordant and upsetting notes surely
give the Magpie its bad reputation.

ale

Female

Juvenile

5 cm. 80-100 g.
see Starling, page 412.

Fieldfare

Turdus pilaris

Across Middle and Northern Europe, Fieldfares nest
small, loose groups. They are large, bold thrushes, as
as Blackbirds, but with a much more striking pattern
Their white under wings are obvious in flight and, as
they fly away, and so is the grey rump contrasting wi
broad, black tail.

In spring the chest becomes a deep golden-buff,
verging on orange, and the black spots on the breast
flanks merge into large dark patches. A spring Fieldfa
is an eye-catching bird.

In autumn, Fieldfares gather and move south and we
large, straggling flocks. This is when they are best knov
likewise on through winter and early spring, as they ro
the fields and hedgerows, and roost in heathland thicke
often in the company of Redwings. At first, they feed o
berries in the hawthorns, but once these are exhausted,
they turn to the fields, where they search energetically f
worms. They bounce across the ground like so many
Blackbirds on a lawn. At the least disturbance they are
flying to the nearest tall hedge or tree, decorating the u
branches like a litter of torn paper blowing in the wind
giving their distinctive, chuckling *chak-chak-chak* calls.
the coast is clear, they come down again, a few at a tim
spread over the ploughed ground or meadow and resu
searching for food.

Fieldfare

Sparrow

N and C, April - Sept.
C and W, Sept - May.

cm. 80-130 g.
see Mistle Thrush, page 334.

Song Thrush
Turdus philomelos

Dawn comes early in spring and the loud, strident no
of a Song Thrush on the roof can be beautiful or a
nuisance, depending on your point of view. Many are
indeed strident and shouted, rather than musical, but
others are as rich and perfect as any note from any
European songster. To prove that the song was no flu
the thrush repeats it again and again: it is the two, th
or four times repetition of short phrases that separate
the song from that of the Blackbird.

Song Thrushes eat worms, typically found from a
spacious, mossy, not-so-perfect lawn, but in dry spells
summer they need a supplementary diet of snails. The
they smash with a loud thwack against a stone or gar
slab. Modern farming techniques, dry summers and o
factors conspire against the thrushes, which do better
damp wooded places than in exposed, easily desiccate
agricultural regions where food is hard to find.

Song Thrushes are small, neat thrushes with lines of
shaped spots on a bright buff breast: the bigger Mistle
Thrush (page 334) is greyer and has bold, rounded spo
on a more uniformly pale underside. Female Blackbirds
sometimes a bit spotty below, but never so pale a brow
a Song Thrush, so there is little room for confusion.

Song Thrush

Sparrow

In N and E,
summer only.

Adult

Juvenile

m. 70-90 g.
see Mistle Thrush, page 334.

Redwing

Turdus iliacus

On a dark October night, with stars sharp and bright listen for the calls of birds flying invisibly above you. The thin, persistent, confident *seeep* of passing Redwi can be heard all over Britain and many parts of Nort western Europe, as these small northerly thrushes mo south and west for the winter.

The Redwing is a small, dark thrush, not much big than a Starling: a little scrap of a bird for such long ar determined travels. It can be told most easily by the be cream stripes on its head, above and below a dark che patch, but also has a much more distinctive under side than a Song Thrush, with long, dark streaks. Redwing are much more social, too, often with Fieldfares in wir when flocks roam the fields and hedges eating berries searching for worms. As the season moves on, so they become more restricted to fields, especially old grassy pastures. In severe weather they may come to gardens but they are not typically garden birds.

Despite their long distance wanderings, they are susceptible to the effects of hard weather. Heavy snow may see large numbers of Redwings, Fieldfares, Skylar Lapwings and other birds heading westwards in massi 'hard weather movements', but with recent milder winters, such dramatic happenings have become much less frequent.

Redwing

Sparrow

Moves S and W
in winter.

m. 60-70 g.
see Song Thrush, page 330.

Mistle Thrus

Turdus viscivorus

This is the biggest European thrush, pale and rather greyish, with pale-edged wing feathers, white sides to th tail and eye-catching white under wings. The under side uniformly cream-buff with a liberal scattering of big, bl. rounded or crescent-shaped spots, whereas the smaller Song Thrush has a more obvious whiter belly, browner flanks and V-shaped spots aligned in rows. Juvenile Mis Thrushes have pale spots over the back.

Mistle Thrushes are rather bold in their actions, with long, leaping hops and fast, direct flight, but quite shy except when nesting: a Song Thrush may slip away into nearest hedge when disturbed, but the longer-winged M Thrush is likely to go far away above tree top height.

In spring, a Mistle Thrush has a superb loud, wild, carolling song, not so rigidly structured as a Song Thrus nor so varied as a Blackbird's. It has a beautiful quality never more so than on a wild day swept by squalls and showers of stinging rain.

Mistle Thrushes are aggressive birds, often in pairs, chasing other birds from their nesting territories, and re to take on a cat or even a human intruder. In winter, a Mistle Thrush will use a great deal of energy to defend bush heavy with berries for its own exclusive use. In autumn, however, you might see groups of ten, 20 or m feeding on rowan berries and roaming the open fields.

Mistle Thrush

Sparrow

Leaves N and E
in winter.

m. 110-140 g.
see Song Thrush, page 330.

Cetti's Warble

Cettia cetti

A sudden, loud outburst comes from somewhere clos
a ditch, stream, or pool: whichever, the bird responsi
is hidden in a thicket of willow or bramble, or deep
within reeds or tall grasses and sedge. For a minute, y
scrutinise the spot in case it should show itself: only f
the explosive outburst to be repeated from a different
area altogether. So the 'chase' goes on: this is the Cet
Warbler, as elusive as they come.

The song is rich and full-throated: *cheee! cheee!
cheweee chewee chewee-wee-wee-o*! Once heard, it is
more or less unmistakable. Occasionally, it also make
loud, sharp *zwik* call, or quieter *squit* call. The bird k
its head down, but with care and patience it might be
seen because it can reveal itself quite clearly, often in a
willow or bramble bush. It looks like a stocky, thickse
rich red-brown warbler, paler beneath, with a white st
over the eye. If lucky you might see its rounded tail, w
bars on the coverts beneath, which clinch its identity.

Cetti's Warblers move northwards during milder
periods, but retreat after harsh, frosty winters, which
take a severe toll on this resident species. They like
tangled, bushy thickets close to reeds and open water
and the spread of flooded gravel pits has offered ther
many new opportunities.

Cetti's Warbler

Sparrow

All year.

n. 10-18 g.
ee Reed Warbler, page 342.

Grasshopper Warbler

Locustella naevia

This bird is a useful test of high frequency deafness: many people lose the ability to hear the song as they g older. Though not musical, nor in any sense a virtuosc performance, it is remarkable: a sharp, metallic, very fast, slightly rattling trill, the notes more distinct at cl range, running together into a long, even reel at a distance. This can continue for some minutes without break, the only variation being an apparent change in pitch and volume as the singer turns its head. It has a curiously mechanical quality, hardly like a bird at all.

The song is given from inside a low bush grown through with tall grass, and if you hear it, this is by f the best chance of seeing a Grasshopper Warbler. Otherwise, the bird keeps down in thick cover, creepi about like a mouse between the stems. It needs rough ground with rank, unkempt grass where people, as a whole, don't often stray. As the countryside becomes more tidy, neat and acceptable, Grasshopper Warbler become scarcer. A few survive on the drier edges of r beds and on moors with little patches of rushes and bracken. In winter, like most European warblers, it migrates to Africa.

Grasshopper Warbler

Sparrow

April to September.

n. 11-15 g.

see Sedge Warbler, page 340.

Sedge Warble

Acrocephalus schoenobaenus

The fidgety, irascible nature of the Sedge Warbler seem
to fit well the untidy, rough nature of its waterside
habitat: it likes nettles, dense brambles, banks of
umbellifers and comfrey, hawthorns and willows in an
around beds of reeds and reedmace, by lakes, pits,
streams or rivers.

In places with reeds it is often found alongside the
Reed Warbler and the two songs are worth learning. 7
Reed makes a rhythmic, chuntering, comfortable soun
while the Sedge Warbler's song is more varied and
scolding in quality. It often starts with several sweet, p
musical notes before 'descending' into the fast chatter
is so characteristic. The two sing most determinedly
around dawn: a reed bed dawn chorus is quite drama

Sedge Warblers also look more silvery-white beneat
and have dull streaks above, but the obvious feature i
broad creamy stripe over each eye. Young birds have
pale crown strripe, and faint streaks on the chest. The
Reed Warbler is plainer overall.

Unlike the resident Cetti's Warbler, which may also
inhabit similar places, the Sedge is a summer visitor to
Europe, spending the winter in West Africa. During
migration, in spring and especially autumn, it is quite
common in damp, marshy areas, particularly along
coasts. It is not a garden bird and has to be sought ou

Sedge Warbler

Sparrow

Most of Europe,
April to September.

n. 10-13 g.
see Reed Warbler, page 342.

Reed Warble

Acrocephalus scirpaceus

Like the Bearded Tit, this is a species linked closely w
reeds, but the connection is a little less rigid. Some b.
in other vegetation, such as reed grass and reedmace,
many feed in and around willows, even singing from
willow bushes. Nevertheless, most prefer more pure
stands of reed, and the species is therefore very locali
within its wide range.

In late April, Reed Warblers suddenly appear and
begin to sing, using a relatively even, rhythmic song
pattern with much repetition, such as *chrree chrree*,
churr churr churr, chirrip chirrip chirrip. The overall
churring, buzzing quality is obvious. The singer gras
an upright stem and sits there, just below the tops of
reeds. In thin reeds you can get a clear view, but in d
reeds it can be frustratingly hard to see.

Reed Warblers are plain, pale, rufous-brown birds
lighter underneath, with just a weak paler line over t
eye. They look slim, rather tapered, with quite long,
spiky bills and low foreheads adding to the effect. Th
are several other species in Europe that look similar,
this is the most common, most widespread and most
easily seen of the plain brown reed bed birds.

Reed Warbler

Sparrow

April to September.

m. 10-15 g.
see Sedge Warbler, page 340.

Icterine & Melodious Warbler

Hippolais icterina and *Hippolais polyglotta*

There are several small green warblers in Europe, most in the genus *Phylloscopus* – for example the Willow Warbler and Chiffchaff. These two are in the genus *Hippolais*, which may seem an obscure thought, but is important, as the whole character of these birds is distinctive. They have stronger legs and feet, much broader-based, spike-like, pale bills, plainer-looking heads and squarer tails. They tend to crash about clumsily, rather than sliding softly through foliage.

The **Icterine** is the more easterly, the **Melodious** more westerly in Europe, meeting in France. They like light woods, rambling hedges with taller trees and leafy orchards. Both are rare, usually autumn, migrants on U.K. coasts, Icterines mostly in the east, Melodious in the south-west. Inland, in the U.K., they are almost unknown.

They are green and yellow, basically, but fade brown or greyer, and some juveniles are very grey-brown and buff. Telling them apart is difficult, but the Icterine has a more peaked crown, the Melodious a rounder head. More important, the Icterine has longer wings, creating a long wing tip point when closed over the tail, and a more obvious, bolder pale panel along the middle of the closed wing. Both have fast, slightly rambling, chattering song in spring, and the Melodious often calls with short note like a Sparrow's.

Icterine Warbler

Sparrow

April to October.

Icterine Warbler

Melodious Warbler

Melodious Warbler

Sparrow

species 13 cm. 11-14 g.
see Willow Warbler, page 360.

April to September.

Subalpine Warbler

Sylvia cantillans

The group of warblers in the genus *Sylvia* are all busy, quite bright little birds, with a perky shape often emphasized by a slightly raised tail. In the Mediterranean region there are several that are not found much farther north, and the Subalpine is one of the smallest, most active and most widely spread.

It likes the typical low, aromatic Mediterranean scrub with plenty of thorns and spiny leaves, and little bushy thickets, but is also often found in prickly hedges around small fields. It is not so familiar around houses and in hotel grounds as the bolder Sardinian Warbler.

The Subalpine looks like a small Whitethroat in some ways, but is quite different in colour. The male is pale bluish-grey above, browner on the wings, with a white-sided tail and white belly. The chin, throat and upper breast are a rich, pale pinkish-red, and the white streak from the bill under the cheek is characteristic. Females and young birds are somewhat browner, duller, and much less pink below, with the white moustachial stripe still there, but much less contrasted against the paler chin.

Subalpine Warblers have a fast, buzzy, chattering song with little musical quality or distinct shape, but characteristic of this group. It is often given in a brief song flight.

Subalpine Warbler

Sparrow

March to October.

Spring male

Female

m. 12-15 g.
see Whitethroat, page 350.

Lesser Whitethroa

Sylvia curruca

In late April, the Lesser Whitethroat returns from Afr
via the Middle East: its migration route is more easte
than other warblers'. Its presence is usually noted wh
its song floats across from the edge of a wood or a
dense, old hedgerow. It is, above all, a bird of thicket
such as blackthorn or hawthorn.

The song is simple but distinct, with a rather hard,
hollow, wooden quality, a short, even rattle on one n
chika-chika-chika-chika-chika. Closer, a short, subdue
introductory warble can be heard. Like several relate
warblers, such as the Blackcap, it has hard, abrupt ca
but it can produce a very high, thin metallic zip which
different, if not often heard.

This is a neat little bird and the even cleaner, brigh
juveniles are particularly smart in autumn. The upper
side is dull grey-brown, the under side whiter, with a
of pink. Its head is grey, contrasting with a clean whi
throat. At certain angles, the area around the eye and
cheek looks a little darker. Unlike the chestnut-winge
Common Whitethroat, it has dull wings, but it shares
long tail with white sides. A useful aid to identificatio
the dark colour of the legs, whereas the Whitethroat's
are pale pink.

Lesser Whitethroat

Sparrow

Most of Europe,
April to September.

Spring male

Juvenile

m. 10-15 g.
see Whitethroat, page 350.

Whitethroa

Sylvia communis

For decades, Whitethroats were among the commones
small countryside birds, but in the 1960s this pleasing
abundance ended with a sudden 'crash' – numbers fell
three quarters or more and this busy, fussy little bird o
hedgerows, bramble brakes and nettlebeds became qui
rare. The cause was a drought in Africa and a widenin
the Sahara: yet the Whitethroat, which must cross this
desert twice each year, has somehow adapted and retu
to thrive in many of its old favourite places.

While both sexes have a white throat, only the male
the more distinguished grey head. Usually, the splash o
bright rusty-brown on the wings and the long, white-e
tail are the most helpful markings for telling it from ot
small warblers. Juveniles are browner than adults, wit
wings edged ginger. Females are browner than males, v
a pale grey-brown head. The Lesser Whitethroat (page
348) has dull grey-brown wings and much blacker legs

The cock bird, often shuffling about deep in low
vegetation and flicking his tail, frequently bursts into s
This is more effort and ambition than achievement, as
amounts merely to a buzzy, scratchy warble, often wit
rhythmic effect. In his excitement, he will perch on an
overhead wire or sing in a fluttery display flight, befor
diving down to stay out of sight for a few minutes, unt
his irrepressible energy demands another burst of song

Whitethroat

Sparrow

April to September.

Adult male

n. 14-18 g.
see Lesser Whitethroat, page 348.

Garden Warbler

Sylvia borin

Not all bird names convey an accurate impression and this small, rather plain warbler is not a bird of garden. It turns up, now and then, in autumn, coming in for i share of honeysuckle or elderberries, but it never uses feeders or birdtables and needs larger areas of woodl and bushy thickets than modern gardens usually offer

It is a migrant from Africa, arriving later in spring than the Blackcap, adding its song to the dawn choru similar places, but it can cope with bushier areas with fewer trees. It has a fine song, not quite first rank, bu rich and flowing, with a conversational style. It usual lacks the panache of a Blackcap, but often the two so are hard to distinguish. Once seen, the Garden Warbl seems a plain little bird, but, like most, has a charm c its own: the large, dark eye, a hint of grey on the necl and, otherwise, a lack of obvious features make it curiously distinctive.

What makes it a typical warbler rather than some other small, brown bird such as a flycatcher? Look at way it moves: though not the lightest and most agile its group, it still slips easily through foliage, more or horizontal, neither very upright nor particularly acrobatic. Only rarely does it stay more than a few moments on the ground.

Garden Warbler

Sparrow

April to October.

n. 15-20 g.
see Blackcap, Spotted Flycatcher, pages 354 and 366.

Blackcap

Sylvia atricapilla

Although its name offers no clue, this is a warbler, similar to several species in southern Europe, but less likely to be mistaken for any other farther north. It i however, more often heard than seen, and its voice m to be distinguished with care from the Garden Warbl Most European warblers migrate to Africa in winter, many Blackcaps remain in southern Europe and even few are scattered through Britain, where they tend to dominate garden feeders.

In spring and summer, the Blackcap reveals its bes side. The male has a richly beautiful song, whose full throated, musical quality is almost unrivalled, but th phrases are short, not nearly so sustained as the song a Nightingale or Blackbird. The notes come fast, tumbling out in a stream, gaining both pace and vol before a typically rather abrupt stop. The song of a Garden Warbler tends to be more even in pace and rambles on a little longer.

Male Blackcaps have black caps, and are otherwis greyish. Females and young birds are browner, and h small caps of a dull chestnut. In spring, they like woo and parks with thick undergrowth and Blackcap son typical of large wooded gardens and orchards, and th edges of broad-leaved woodland clearings. In autumn Blackcaps fatten up on sugary fruits, such as elderbe

Blackcap

Sparrow

Mostly March to September, but a few all year in S and W.

Female

Male

ח. 15-20 g.
ee Marsh Tit, page 374.

Wood Warble

Phylloscopus sibilatrix

Warm, calm and sunny days in early April stretch the
patience of the birdwatcher wanting a Wood Warbler.
But the bird can't be hurried and arrives, in its own ti
towards the end of the month. Then, when the mornii
sun shines brilliantly through fresh beech leaves and o
buds and foliage appear in a froth of yellow-green and
pink, the sudden song is heard: a hesitant, tinny little
stutter that runs into a fast silvery trill. Every eight or
songs, there will be two or three quite different sweet,
sad phrases, something like *sioo-sioo-sioo-sioo*. Few
birds have two such distinct song types. At this time t
Wood Warbler is most easily seen, before the canopy
becomes complete and too dense. They tend to go
directly to and from their nesting woods and are rare
seen as migrants elsewhere.

Wood Warblers, redstarts and Pied Flycatchers are
often linked, all preferring woods with a closed canoi
letting in little light, so the ground is clear of all but
swathe of bluebells. Wood Warblers nest on the grou
but feed and sing up in the trees.

Apart from the distinctive song, they can be told fi
the much commoner Willow Warbler by their greene
upper side and whiter under side, with a flush of yell
on the throat, a bolder stripe over the eye and yellow
green feather edges on the longer wings and tail.

Wood Warbler

Sparrow

April to September.

n. 8-13 g.
see Willow Warbler, page 360.

Chiffchaff

Phylloscopus collybita

In March, one of the earliest migrants to north-western
Europe from Africa reappears and begins to sing straigh
away, often from a waterside clump of willows, where th
will be the best supply of insect food at this early stage o
spring. Later the bird moves to the tops of tall trees with
thick undergrowth. Many Chiffchaffs spend the winter i
southern Europe, and a very few in the north-west, but
arrival in spring is nevertheless eagerly anticipated, a full
month before the Swallow or Cuckoo.

Chiffchaff

Sparrow

Chiffchaffs are small, pale, brownish birds with a hin
green; beneath, they are a light, parchment colour. They
look very like Willow Warblers, but have tiny, blackish
and a more or less marked little half ring of white unde
each eye, rounder heads and subtly shorter wings – but
none of these are especially obvious. More useful is the
frequent down-up bob of the tail as they feed. The song
an instant giveaway, a simple repetition of three or four
short, sharp notes in seemingly random order, *chiff-cha*
chiff-chaff-chep-chaff-chup-chiff-chaff.

Close-up you can hear an occasional little, low churr
note, too. The song penetrates the woodland canopy an
can be heard from passing cars on noisy roads: it is clea
made for long-range communication between Chiffcha
meaning, like all bird songs, 'I'm here, this is my patch,
out unless you are an unattached female: if so, come ov

Mostly March to
October.

Juvenile – yellower than adult

n. 7-9 g.
see Willow Warbler, page 360.

Willow Warble

Phylloscopus trochilus

Willow Warbler

Sparrow

Mostly April to September. In S, only April, or Aug - Sept.

It is late April: a warm day with sunshine and little wi
Go down to a river valley, with its thicket of willow a
birch growing from the mixture of peat and gravelly s
The Willow Warblers should be back, fresh from Afric
At this time, the song seems the most delicate, most
lyrical, sweetest sound. It is not a heavyweight in the
birdsong performances, but the light, simple phrase th
swells, falls away and ends with a flourish is a perfect
companion to the new greens of spring woodland.

Willow Warblers are widespread, but declining in
many areas where the Chiffchaff seems to be doing
better. It is not clear why, and the habitat needs of the
two sometimes overlap. Neither are really garden bir
but both may be found in parks, old railway cuttings
similar suburban situations.

Willow Warblers look exceedingly like Chiffchaffs
are a difficult identification challenge unless they are
singing. Both are not quite green, not quite brown, m
the colour of pale, bleached oak bark, with a paler
underside and light stripe over the eye. Willow Warbl
generally have pale legs, Chiffchaffs dark. In summer,
young ones of both species look greenish and yellowis
Willow Warblers are a little longer and sleeker, and ca
with a distinct *hoo-eet*, whereas Chiffchaffs slur *hwee*

Autumn juvenile.
Much yellower than adult

n. 7-9 g.
see Chiffchaff, Wood Warbler, pages 358 and 356.

Goldcrest
Regulus regulus

Goldcrests are year-round birds over most of Europe, there is something about them that is especially appea in autumn and winter. Perhaps it is because they migr. across the North Sea and make landfall on remote coastlines in all kinds of weather, tiny mites – the tinie birds in all of Europe – that take little or no notice of people. Their thin, sibilant *see-see-see* calls evoke the shortening days of autumn to perfection, especially fr some dark, dense conifer of the kind Goldcrests espec prefer. On the gloomiest of days, in the darkest yew h or pine, the pale olive-green of a Goldcrest seems alm to glow, so clean and light does it look, dull black and whitish zig-zag wing bars and a thin streak of yellow the crown adding the final touches that also help iden it. Juveniles lack colour on the crown.

Goldcrest song disappears from many people's hear with age: it is a test of high pitch sensitivity. If you ca hear it, you will soon recognize the fast, repeated rhyt of the short phrase, with a flourish at the end – *tid-ee ee tid-ee tid-ee teedle-di-dee*. The nest is a minute hammock of moss and cobweb, slung beneath a spray pine or spruce or some ornamental, exotic conifer: eve a largely broad-leaved wood, it is the tall, isolated conifers that act as magnets for this little bird.

Goldcrest

Sparrow

All Europe except
far N.

. 5-7 g.

see Firecrest, page 364.

Firecrest

Regulus ignicapilla

In size, shape and form, the Firecrest is a twin of the
Goldcrest. Over mainland Europe, it is almost as
widespread, but rarely so common; in Britain, it is a
rare breeding bird and in most places just an occasion
stray in autumn and winter. It likes tall conifers and
thickets of pine and holly, but migrants and wintering
Firecrests also go for lower, bushy tangles of willow,
holly and ivy.

The call is much like a Goldcrest's and not always
easy to distinguish: a little firmer, less often grouped
short sequences, more *zit* than *seep*: but Goldcrests c
call that way, too. The song is more reliable (althoug
there is a frustrating tendency for mimicry in this pai
zi-zi-zi-zi-zi-zeee rather than *tidl-dee tidl-dee*, accelera
and gaining strength before finishing without the flou
of a Goldcrest's song.

Against the sky it can look just like a Goldcrest, bu
least with a hint of a stronger head pattern. A better
will reveal brighter green above, white under parts, a
of golden-bronze about the shoulder, and a unique he
pattern: a black cap split by a central line of orange o
yellow, a bold white wedge over the eye and a thin da
eye stripe, quite unlike the open, plain-faced look of a
Goldcrest. It is, indeed, a beautiful little creature, a ge

Firecrest

Sparrow

Mainly in S and W.
Rare in Britain.

5-7 g.

see Goldcrest, page 362.

Spotted Flycatcher

Muscicapa striata

In most of north-western Europe, it is not until late M
even June, that the Spotted Flycatcher arrives from Af
In recent years, it has been seen in diminishing numbe
It likes clearings between tall trees, at woodland edges
parks, around cemeteries and tennis courts, or in
relatively rural gardens. It finds perches, from a post o
gravestone up to a high tree top, from which it watche
for flying insects. Sunshine across a clearing, against a
dark background, catches the glint of a fly. The flycato
darts out, twists and snatches the prey in its bill, then
instantly returns to its perch, to sit upright, on very sh
legs, still and attentive. Its big, bright eye is ideal for t
task, and lends an intelligent, alert expression that hel
make this dull brown bird an appealing character.

Together with the short legs and an upright stance,
pale plumage with buff feather edges marking the long
wings, and paler, almost silvery underside with faint
dusky chest streaks, add up to a distinctive character,
contrast to the warblers that tend to shuffle horizonta
through foliage.

Spotted Flycatchers nest in broken stumps or other
small hollows, and take advantage of hanging baskets,
coconut shells placed in creepers or old blackbird nests
they like a low threshold, over which they can see whil
incubating eggs, and fly off in a moment if disturbed.

Spotted Flycatcher

Sparrow

May to September.

. 14-18 g.
ee Garden Warbler, Pied Flycatcher, pages 352 and 368.

Pied Flycatcher

Ficedula hypoleuca

Pied Flycatcher

Sparrow

Much of N and W
Europe, April to
October.

Pied Flycatchers are intensely territorial, so much so
they even set up temporary territories when they pau
Spain while migrating north from Africa in spring. I
north-western Europe, they breed in oak woodland,
in managed woods with little dead or dying timber, t
numbers can be increased if nestboxes are provided.

Pied Flycatchers drop to the ground to pick up ins
but most they catch in the air in small clearings, or in
the woodland canopy. Unlike Spotted Flycatchers, the
rarely double back to the same perch. Males are supe
black and white, with bold white wing patches and a
single or double white spot over the bill. Females hav
same pattern, but in brown and white. Autumn birds
sullied below, with quite strong dusky stripes each si
the throat. These turn up in unexpected places and
regularly in woods and thickets close to the coast, oft
when other migrants, such as redstarts, are in evidenc

In places such as Gotland in the Baltic, and in sou
eastern Europe, there are closely related species, Col
and Semi-collared Flycatchers. These are difficult to
identify, but, those apart, the Pied Flycatcher is a
distinctive bird. The difficulty is finding it in dense
foliage, especially in late summer when they seem to
disappear from their nesting places.

Male

Female

1. 10-15 g.
ee Spotted Flycatcher, page 366.

Bearded & Penduline Tits

Panurus biarmicus and *Remiz pendulin*

There are several European birds that are remarkably restricted in their choice of habitat, and the **Bearded T** one: it needs reed beds, and that's the end of the matte winter, some disperse and end up in sedge and reedma beds, but only temporarily – in spring they return to th reeds. To nest successfully, they need a layer of dry lea litter at the base of the reeds, plus access to small pool find sufficient insects for their brood. Reed beds natur tend to dry out, so Bearded Tits thrive best where the reeds are managed, on nature reserves. On a breezy da you might hear their loud, pinging *dink-dink* calls but find it hard to see one. Calmer weather offers better opportunities to appreciate the rich colours of these sr long-tailed birds with their sharp, waxy yellow bills.

In winter, the **Penduline Tit** is a bird of reed beds, especially in mixed fenland. It keeps low, or perches on reedmace head and pulls out the seeds. In spring, it me to river sides, ditches or marshy areas with an abunda of willows and poplars. There, it tears at the feathery flower heads and uses the down from the catkins to b remarkable nests, suspended from thin, drooping twig

It is a small bird, not very closely related to other tit but equally agile. It looks pale grey and red-brown, wi dark patch through the eye like a tiny shrike. The best to locate it is to follow its call: a simple, high, *ps-eeeee*

Bearded Tit

Sparrow

All year, but scattered.

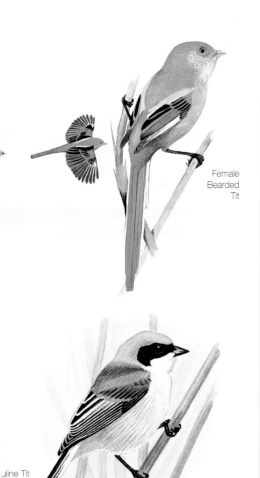

Female
Bearded
Tit

Penduline Tit

Sparrow

uline Tit

ed: 17 cm. 13-20 g.
uline: 11 cm. 9-12 g.
e Reed Warbler, Red-backed Shrike, pages 342 and 392.

All year. Slowly
spreading to W.

Long-tailed Tit
Aegithalos caudatus

Family parties or related groups of Long-tailed Tits g[...]
together and spend their days wandering through tre[...]
and hedgerows, communicating with quiet contact n[...]
and moving single file from place to place in long,
straggling lines. You can often find them by listening
their abrupt, dry *tup tup* or *trrrp trrp* notes, mixed w[...]
high, thin, formless *seee-seee* calls. These are someth[...]
like Goldcrest calls, but have less shape, or emphasis

Long-tailed Tits often perch close together, even cud[...]
up tight side by side, unlike most birds, which keep th[...]
distance. They have interesting social behaviour and
nesting pairs may be assisted by 'helpers', usually brot[...]
of the breeding male bird. Females seem to disperse m[...]
widely. The nest, usually quite low in a bramble, gorse[...]
bush or blackthorn thicket, is a miracle of engineering[...]
enclosed, egg-shaped flask of moss, spider's webs, feat[...]
and lichens. These materials are very elastic, allowing
nest to expand as the brood of chicks develops inside.
They can give perfect camouflage, but a bleached, whi[...]
nest can sometimes be surprisingly obvious.

Until recently, Long-tailed Tits were not garden bi[...]
and did not come to feeders, but they have learned t[...]
so and take shreds of peanuts from hanging baskets,
from the ground beneath. These feeding groups are
delightful to watch.

Long-tailed Tit

Sparrow

Most of Europe,
all year.

Adult.
Juvenile lacks
pink and is
blacker above

n. 8-9 g.

Marsh & Willow Tits

Parus palustris and Parus montan

These two are virtually identical, renowned for being difficult to separate. Both are small, stocky, large-hea woodland tits, with small bills and moderately long ta and both are dull brown and black, with no trace of blue, green or yellow. They are, however, easily separa from the Blackcap by their calls, shape and black chin

The **Marsh Tit** is marginally the smarter of the two, **Willow** fractionally the more colourful. Marsh Tits ha smoother, shinier caps. The Willow Tit's cap extends a little further back. The Willow has slightly chubbier, whiter cheeks (much whiter on the greyer birds of Scandinavia) and a slightly rougher, larger bib. The Willow looks chunkier, more bull-necked, and has a rounder tail. The best plumage feature is usually a pa band along the closed wing on the Willow (but neithe have a pale bar across it), and Willows in southern ar western Europe tend to look brighter on the flanks th the pale, grey Marsh Tit. In the north, they are grey, whiter beneath.

If you hear a bright, sharp, clearly enunciated *pit-chew*, it is a Marsh Tit: no difficulty. A deep, nasal, buzzy *nair-nair-nair* or *eez-eez-eez* comes from a Will but beware the lighter *chick-a-dee-dee-dee* also commonly heard from a Marsh Tit.

Marsh Tit

Sparrow

All year.

Marsh Tit

Willow Tit

Willow Tit

Sparrow

All year.

sh Tit: 12 cm. 10-12 g.
w Tit: 12 cm. 9-10 g.
see Coal Tit, page 378.

Crested Tit

Parus cristatus

Crested Tits are widespread in Europe, found in a mixture of habitats so long as there are pine trees somewhere. However, in Britain they are restricted entirely to Scots pines in northern Scotland, so there t are rare and special birds, exciting to find.

Superficially, they are like the other brown and bla tits, especially the Marsh Tit, but look smaller-headed and flit about more actively through the canopy of pi They have no trace of brighter colour, instantly ruling out Blue and Great Tits, nor wing bars, which preven confusion with the Coal Tit. The obvious feature is a sharp, pointed crest of black and white feathers; the f has a lacy black pattern on dull white.

Most often, you realize that a Crested Tit is aroun when you hear its distinctive calls. Apart from the us high, sharp tit notes, it makes a dry, purring, rhythmi *pt-chrrr-up*. Patiently follow this through the trees an you will usually get the reward of at least a brief view before the bird moves away through the wood.

Most tits use existing holes to nest in, but the Cres like the Willow, excavates its own hole, usually in a l dead pine stump. Nestboxes filled with sawdust and wood chips can help them where such stumps are few

Crested Tit

Sparrow

All year in UK, continued to N Scotland.

n. 10-14 g.
see Coal Tit, Marsh Tit, pages 378 and 374.

Coal Tit
Parus ater

If you have a peanut feeder and live close to a wood
some pine trees, you are likely to see a small brown,
black and white bird snatch a nut and make off with
as if it prefers to eat in privacy. This will probably be
Coal Tit. It also takes food away for hiding, in order
have a store for later – perhaps when it turns cold.

Crows hide food and remember exactly where the
put it. Coal Tits seem to put bits of food into places
they are likely to search anyway, so come across their
little caches by chance, often in secret spots such as t
spaces between tufts of pine needles. They usually lo
in confined places for seeds, insects, spiders and spid
eggs – they feed on small items, little but often.

Coal Tits have no green, blue or yellow in their
plumage like some of the other tits, but they do have
noticeably bold white cheeks and a distinctive white
rectangle on the back of the largely black head. They
like Great Tits but make a higher, squeakier sound, a
befits a much smaller bird – indeed, this is one of
Europe's tiniest. You can also hear odd little spitting
at close quarters, but the song is bright and cheery, a
repetitive *tsee-oo tsee-oo tsee-oo*.

Coal Tit

Sparrow

Most of Europe,
all year.

Yellowish cheeks
in Ireland

ndinavian form

cm. 8-10 g.
see Great Tit, page 382.

Blue Tit
Parus caeruleus

A Blue Tit is such a small scrap of life that it seems to dart full speed across a garden and stop dead, as if stuck firm to a hanging feeder. There is no acceleration or deceleration with such a small, light creature – it is all nothing, full speed or stopped.

Life is like that for a Blue Tit: highly strung, a bag of nerves, forever on the look-out for a Sparrowhawk, or cat. Blue Tits are generally abundant, and frequent prey of predators. They breed best in woodland, where there is an abundance of caterpillars in spring; those that nest in boxes in gardens produce fewer young, as natural foods are much scarcer there.

After a single brood early in the year, Blue Tit families get together in roaming, semi-nomadic flocks that wander through woods and gardens, unwittingly exploiting the theory that many eyes are better than one. Many birds are more likely than one or two to find food and much more likely to see approaching danger. Such flocks are often mixed with bigger Great Tits and Chaffinches, and smaller Coal Tits and Goldcrests. The Blue Tits, with their blue caps, white faces and blue wings and tails, are easily identified. They are familiar favourites at the bird feeder, eager to take peanuts and sunflower seeds.

Blue Tit

Sparrow

All but far N,
all year.

Adult

Juvenile

m. 9-14 g.
see Great Tit, page 382.

Great Tit

Parus major

Great Tits herald spring as vigorously as any other songster, shouting a strident, repetitive, two-note song through woods, parks and gardens. It is a sharp, metal *tea-cher tea-cher tea-cher*, with many variations in pitch speed and emphasis. Indeed, the Great Tit has a large vocabulary apart from its song, with more than 30 recognized calls. If you hear a strange bird call in a wood, likely as not it is made by a Great Tit.

This is a large, stocky bird compared with the tiny Blue and Coal Tits that often associate with it. It is generally common, easy to see and attracted to garden feeders, which it dominates with its forceful character. Where smaller tits feed in tiny outer twigs, Great Tits often concentrate on bigger branches and the bole of a tree, and pick up fallen seeds from the ground below.

Like other tits, it nests in holes in trees ready made woodpeckers, or formed by fallen branches. It also uses holes in walls and nestboxes.

This is an easy bird to identify, with plenty of blue-grey, yellow and black, and a big white patch on each side of the head. The yellow under side has a dark central stripe, narrowing downwards on females but broadening out on older males. The Blue Tit, in comparison, has just a broken, thin pencil line.

Great Tit

Sparrow

All Europe, all year.

Immature

Adult

. 16-21 g.
ee Blue Tit, Coal Tit, pages 380 and 378.

Nuthatch

Sitta europaea

A clue to the whereabouts of a Nuthatch is a hole in
tree, or a nestbox, plastered round with dried mud.
Nuthatches can't resist this bit of building work, eve
the hole is about the right size. Any nest hole that is
little larger than the body width will be converted to
snug fit by means of a little plasterwork.

Nuthatches, in any case, call often and once you k
their various loud trills and boyish whistles, you hea
more than you ever see. They like large parks and
woodlands with big, old trees such as beeches and li
but avoid coniferous woods. When you see one, the
low-slung shape, dagger bill and flat head, short squ
tail and short legs give it a distinctive shape, even if
can't see the colour up against the sky. A close view
reveals blue-grey above, buff below with rusty-brow
flanks and a thick band of black through the eye.
Scandinavian birds are white underneath.

Nuthatches are nearly always seen on trees, but th
may also explore old walls and quite often come to
ground to hop about in search of fallen berries, seed
and nuts which they will wedge into crevices and th
probe by pecking. They are entertaining when they
bird feeder, adding a shot of life and colour to the u
cast of tits and finches.

Nuthatch

Sparrow

Most of Europe,
all year.

. 20-24 g.
ee Treecreeper, page 388.

Nutcracker
Nucifraga caryocatactes

From the top of a tall pine beside a high Alpine pastur
spindle-shaped object, pointed at each end, drops almo
vertically towards the ground. Suddenly it sprouts win
and shoots off across a clearing, heading for more tree
nearby, where it shoots upwards to a new, exposed pe
This is the Nutcracker: buoyant, energetic, bouncy.

It is Jackdaw sized, but generally a dark, rich brow
with copious long white spots all over, sometimes, in
fresh plumage, almost concealing the brown beneath.
the feathers become older, the white wears off a little
has a glossy, grey-black cap, blackish wings and a bro
white area around the tail. The big, dagger-shaped,
shiny black bill is distinctive, too. Sometimes over-
enthusiastic people mistake a Starling or a young Mi
Thrush for a Nutcracker.

A specialist pine seed feeder, the Nutcracker is firm
centred on Alpine and northern forests, but sometim
numbers are high and the food supply fails, they hav
move out, looking for food wherever they can find it
These population 'eruptions' are few and far betwee
not nearly so frequent as those of, for example, cros
or Waxwings. So, in far Western Europe, including
Britain, Nutcrackers remain great rarities, not seen f
years at a time.

Nutcracker

Sparrow

All year.

, 110-190 g.
ee Starling, page 412.

Treecreeper & Short-toed Treecreeper

Certhia familiaris and *Certhia brachya[...]*

All day, every day, the **Treecreeper** creeps about on tr[...] it can do little else. Its long body and short legs just aren't made for hopping about on flat ground and it ventures down there infrequently. It may, for variety, occasionally creep on an old wall or a bit of rock. It perfectly adapted for its role in life, with long, curve[...] needle-sharp claws, a tail that gives support against a vertical surface and a fine, curved bill, with which it probes and explores every crevice in the bark, in sea[...] of minute spiders and insects, and their eggs or larva[...]

It can hang beneath a branch, but, unlike the Nuthatch, does not come down head first: it tends to begin at the base of a tree and shuffle upwards, befo[...] flying off to the next tree and starting again. That is for a Treecreeper.

In spring, although overlooked by most people, its sweet, rhythmic, repetitive song is frequent in woodlands. The Treecreeper is unlike any other bird except for one, the **Short-toed Treecreeper**: these two make perhaps the most difficult European pair to separate by sight, but their songs and calls are usual[...] distinct. The Treecreeper's has a flowing cadence wi[...] terminal flourish, whicle the Short-toed sings a shor[...] staccato phrase. The Short-toed is restricted to the European mainland, from Iberia to Eastern German[...]

Treecreeper

Sparrow

All year.

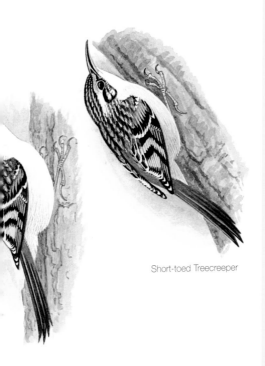

Short-toed Treecreeper

Short-toed Treecreeper

Sparrow

European mainland, Iberia to E Germany.

species: 12.5 cm. 8-11 g

Golden Oriole

Sparrow

Golden Oriole

April to August.

Golden Oriole

Oriolus oriolus

Too often this is merely a voice from the trees: male Golden Orioles sing consistently in spring and summer, especially early in the day and again at dusk, typically from the thick, airy foliage of poplars, or damp, riverside oak woods. Despite their seemingly obvious plumage, in the light and shade and reflections of the leaves they are hard to see, but the song is easily identified. It is too brief to be a great performance, simply two or three notes that flow together with a yodelling effect, but the quality is brilliant, a lovely, full, fluty sound, more or less like *weedl-oo* or *weeloo*. Back off a little, move from side to side to help pinpoint the singer and, with luck, you should see it. Maybe it will quit the trees and fly off to another clump, in which case it will reveal its long, black wings, black tail with a vivid yellow band and the pure, brightest yellow body plumage of any European bird.

Females are harder to see and you need to be sure you have not seen a Green Woodpecker. The Oriole is greenish, paler beneath, with darker wings. It lacks the Green Woodpecker's yellower rump and red crown. Older females look almost as bright as males, but lack the black mark between the bill and eye.

Female

Male

n. 60-80 g.
ee Green Woodpecker, page 270.

Red-backed Shrike

Lanius collurio

Once widespread, but sadly withdrawing from Weste
Europe, and long absent as a breeding bird in Britain
this is Europe's smallest, neatest shrike. It sits upright
often on top of a bush or on a wire, but, like any shr
it can be surprisingly hard to locate. Sometimes one v
sit quietly and almost motionless for long periods. W
feeding, the shrike looks intently at the ground, sway
its tail for balance, then drops down briefly to snatch
beetle, or flies out to catch a bee. It is the large-scale
of such big insects, more than habitat loss, that has d
for the shrike in many of its former sites.

A male is easy to identify, with a black mask across
blue grey head and a black and white tail. Underneath
has a beautiful wash of dog-rose pink. The female is
rufous brown, with a dusky mask, best identified by it
hooked bill, short, dark legs and quite long wings and
It sits much more upright than a Thrush, or the more
secretive Nightingale.

Red-backed Shrikes remain relatively frequent in p
of the north and areas such as the damper, greener
pastures of the mid-altitude Pyrenees. On north-west
European coasts, they remain occasional migrants in
spring and autumn.

Red-backed Shrike

Sparrow

Much of Europe,
April to October.

Female

n. 28-35 g.
see Nightingale, page 312.

Great Grey Shrike

Lanius excubitor

Shrikes are charismatic and have a special presence unu for birds of such small size. The Great Grey Shrike is th biggest and most complicated of them in its racial variations. Those from the south and far east are now treated as a separate species, the Southern Grey Shrike.

The Great Grey is indeed grey, with black and white wings and tail and a white underside. The face is mark by a band of black through the eye, like a pirate's patc Like many simple black, white and grey birds, it can lo extremely handsome.

In winter, shrikes from the north move south and we but are few and far between, always exciting to see. Lil other shrikes, they can be exceptionally elusive: obviou one day, impossible to find the next, but they may han, around for weeks.

They like bushy heaths, but also the edges of conifer plantations adjacent to moors, rough corners of parkla with old trees and riverside thickets with tangles of tho They watch for prey from perches, including overhead wires, but also hover briefly like tiny Kestrels. They ca small rodents such as voles, but also small birds and la insects, sometimes impaling them, or wedging them in forks of twigs for eating later. Impaling also makes the prey convenient for tearing to pieces.

Great Grey Shrike

Sparrow

Much of Europe, all year. N birds move S and W in winter.

m. 50-80 g.
see Magpie, page 400.

Jay

Garrulus glandarius

On the face of it, a Jay seems to have little affinity to crow. But the bill and bristly patch over the nostrils a clue: it is indeed a small, jaunty, colourful crow. Ja vary a little through Europe, with white crowns strea black, or black caps, and greyer or browner backs, b essentially they share the same pattern of pale pink-brown body, black wings and tail and bold white rur The wing has a white patch and a vivid, narrowly-ba azure blue area beyond the joint. This looks obvious book, but is not easily seen except at close range: the black and white patches are usually much more prominent than the azure blue.

Jays are sometimes elusive, and slip away into the of a dense wood with ease, but often their loud, rauc calls – like tearing thick cloth – give away their prese They have other calls, too, including a soft mewing n

At other times, they bound out across the short gra of a park or garden lawn, in a distinctive bouncy wa even visit bird feeders to take nuts. In autumn, they a more obvious in flight over open areas, carrying acor several in the throat, another in the beak – to bury fo eating later. They remember where they bury them, b few inevitably sprout, helping the spread of oak woo

Jay

Sparrow

Most of Europe,
all year.

n. 160 g.
see Hoopoe, page 264.

Siberian Jay

Perisorius infaustus

There is no difficulty in identifying this bird of northe[rn]
forests: it is unique, clearly a Jay in character, with a
small bill and pale, bristly nostrils, a large, broad hea[d]
and a rather densely-feathered, velvety body. Compar[ed]
with the Jay, it has a longer tail, but otherwise shares [the]
same broad, rounded wing shape in flight and has the
same slightly jerky, flicking, floating action.

Overall, they are dark brownish grey, with a darke[r]
liver-brown cap, but their plumage is enlivened by br[ight]
patches of rich rusty orange on wing, rump and tail. [The]
whole underside of the tail is pale orange, often evide[nt]
as a bird perches, facing the birdwatcher, on a low tw[ig].

In Europe, Siberian Jays are Scandinavian specialis[ts],
liking dense tracts of old, untouched, uniform forest.
They like such undisturbed places yet, should anyone
camp in the woods, the Siberian Jay is quite likely to
come looking for scraps. Flocks move in silently, but [like]
to squabble when feeding, with various chattering ca[lls].

They get what they can, eating almost anything edi[ble]
and catch more live food than the Jay, including smal[l]
mammals and birds, but the majority of their diet is
composed of seeds, berries and insects. The Siberian J[ay]
is a great hider of seeds, which it then relocates in wi[nter]
when conditions are severe.

Siberian Jay

Sparrow

Much of Scandinavia,
all year.

. 80-100 g.

see Jay, page 396.

Magpie
Pica pica

Magpie

Sparrow

All Europe, all year.

Through Southern Europe, the Magpie is common, and seems to cause no problems: it has always been so, and there is no need to imagine it otherwise. In north-west Europe it suffered, in the past, from intense persecution along with crows and many birds of prey. When persecution lessened, numbers stabilised, and this has been seen by some as a huge and unwanted increase.

The situation has been compounded by other changes. Magpies can thrive on the abundance of dead meat found every day on the roads, and on all kinds of edible rubbish in litter strewn about town and countryside. They hardly have to work hard to find a decent – or indecent – living. Normally, they are insect-eaters, supplementing this diet with whatever they can find or catch, including the odd bird. In spring, they will turn eggs and chicks, too. Increased numbers in suburban areas has put pressure on garden birds. The screaming parent Blackbirds when nests are threatened by Magpie puts nerves on edge, and many come to hate the bird.

Looked at objectively, it is startlingly handsome: beautiful is perhaps too strong a word, although its iridescent colours certainly are. Young birds are similar to adults but duller, and with a short tail at first. With its domed nest of sticks and complex social rituals, this is a fascinating character.

240 g.
ee Jay, page 396.

Chough
Pyrrhocorax pyrrhocorax

Europe's mountains, gorges and coastal cliffs are grac
by this wonderful bird: a small crow, sheeny black w
green and purple gloss, red legs and a curved, red bill
needs to be distinguished from the Alpine Chough in
mountainous areas (its wings and tail look shorter an
square, its bill is red, not yellow); and from the Jackd
around cliffs (Jackdaws have rounder wing tips and
blunter bills).

Choughs fly brilliantly, with great flair and agility,
purely for the fun of it, soaring on outspread, fingere
wings, diving with wing tips swept back, or twirling
twisting around in tight, complicated turns. They sett
with a springy bound, a flirt of the wings and tail, an
loud, stirring, challenging calls that ring around cliffs
and echo across open valleys. The basic call is *chee-o*
or *ki-yaa*, with shorter or longer variants, usually wi
more ringing or twanging quality than a Jackdaw's.

In Alpine valleys Choughs feed on high, close-crop
pastures. They also like grassy habitats, with an
abundance of insects often associated with cattle or
sheep, around some of the wildest, most remote coas
cliffs in Ireland, Scotland and Wales. Here they nest
sea caves, ancient mineshafts or old, tumbledown st
buildings. Despite their aerial ability, they are someti
caught by Peregrines.

Chough

Sparrow

All year in it's
habitats.

. 250 g.
ee Jackdaw, page 404.

Jackdaw
Corvus monedula

If any bird flies simply for enjoyment, it must be the Jackdaw. It hasn't the ebullience and extravagance of Chough, nor does it have the power of a Raven, but Jackdaw – or, rather, Jackdaws, since these are social birds – just gets up in the air and swings round in wi rising arcs, purely for the fun of it. Any breath of wi enough to get them up: they glide and chase, tumble dive, as if they were great masters of the air rather th humble crows.

All the time, too, they are calling: sharp, squeaky, agitated, aggressive or relaxed versions of their basic '*jack*' notes. They are equally at home doing this on around a coastal or inland cliff, a quarry, an enormo old building such as a cathedral, or a simple suburba house with tall chimneys.

In flight, they look like black pigeons, with quite rounded wing tips, not so deeply fingered as a Crow a Rook's, and quick, paddling wingbeats. On the ground, they are distinguished by their pale grey nec blacker caps and short bills. They are smaller than o crows, but in a mixed flock with Rooks, which are common, this size difference is not always obvious v the birds all are seen at different angles and distance

Jackdaw

Sparrow

Mostly all year.

cm. 250 g.
see Hooded Crow, page 408.

Rook

Corvus frugilegus

Early spring sees a resurgence of activity about the rookery, where any number from a handful to a couple hundred pairs of Rooks have made their large, dark nest of sticks in the tops of a clump of trees. Below, the gro will be liberally splashed with white. Often, they nest c to a village street, or beside a church. They steal each other's sticks, fight and chase, and call frequently, with variety of ringing, trumpeting and cawing sounds. The typical caw is one of the countryside's most distinctive and, in its way, pleasing sounds.

Up close, Rooks are handsome creatures, polished with blue and purple, despite the rather grotesquely b parchment face. The bill is long, tapering to a point a the forehead has a steep step, giving a different profil from the flat head of a Carrion Crow, page 408. Ofte obvious, the body feathers are more lax, especially th baggy trousered effect around the thighs.

Rooks eat plenty of grain and can damage a field growing wheat, but in the main they rely on earthwo which they search for diligently in grassy pastures or ploughed fields. They feed in great flocks spread over these fields, often mixed with Jackdaws, Wood Pigeo Stock Doves and town pigeons. If there is a scattering white gulls around, the Rooks make a striking contra

Rook

Sparrow

In S, only winter.

6 cm. 490 g.
see Carrion Crow, page 408.

Carrion/Hooded Crow

Corvus corone

Everyone seems to be against this bird, as if it were ev
personified. But it is just a bird, trying to get by in the
way for which it is naturally fitted, eating just about
anything it can get. That includes eggs and young bir
but the majority of its food consists of small stuff, suc
as beetles and grubs taken from fields, and already de
animals such as rabbits killed on roads.

Crows are sociable rather than solitary, but not nea
so often found in large flocks as the Rook (page 406)
Even so, where a field has been spread with slurry, w
brings up an abundance of worms, there might be sco
even hundreds, of Carrion Crows feeding together.

Crows tend to glide and soar less than Rooks, perh
because they are less social. They look squarer in the
wing and tail, but a distant 'black crow' can be hard
tell for sure. Closer, they can usually be distinguished
their neater appearance, with tighter feathering on the
body and a flatter forehead. We tend to think of bird
side-on cut out shapes, but, three dimensionally, Cro
are broad, hefty, solid creatures – worth your attentio
should you get a close view.

In Scotland, Ireland, Scandinavia, Italy and Eastern
Europe, Carrion Crows are grey and black and know
Hooded Crows: previously treated as a race, but now
ranked as a separate species.

Carrion Crow

Sparrow

Most of Europe,
all year.

Hooded Crow

cm. 570 g.
see Raven, page 410.

Raven

Corvus corax

Black as a lump of Welsh anthracite, the Raven is the
world's biggest, most imposing crow. It is a few
centimetres longer than a Carrion Crow, but that hard[ly]
tells the whole story: while 'twice as big' is misleading[,]
is actually more than twice the weight of a Carrion o[r]
Hooded Crow, and vastly bulkier when seen alongsid[e.]

Because it is all black, to identify it you must rely o[n]
shape and size, backed by behaviour, actions and voic[e.]
More like a giant Rook than a Carrion Crow, it has [a]
longer, more pointed wings and a long, almost diamo[nd]
shaped tail. Its particularly deep, arched bill is suited [to]
its role as an eater of dead meat, such as sheep, deer [and]
rabbits that have succumbed to the harsh conditions [of]
the high moors or bleak cliff tops. In the air, it soars [and]
glides more than any other large crow. And it has one
unique trick: momentarily rolling on to its back in fli[ght.]

Vocally, it calls for attention by a series of loud, ho[llow]
throaty notes, often metallic or even honking, or just [an]
earthy double croak, like *crruk-crruk*. In spring, howe[ver,]
if you can get very close, you might hear a soft, rambl[ing]
'song', almost like a conversation between a pair of
Ravens, with various clicks and hollow popping soun[ds.]

Raven

Sparrow

Not lowlands of
France and Low
Countries. All year.

7 cm. 1,000-1,400 g.
see Carrion Crow, page 408.

Starling
Sturnus vulgaris

Few birds are more familiar than the Starling, yet, in areas where intensive farming has reduced foraging habitat and insect life, it is in severe decline. One of th great features of the Starling is its tendency to form flocks: not just hundreds, or thousands, but sometimes for the night-time roost, in millions. Great, dense, swirling flocks gather near the intended roost site, ofte settling for a while with a far-carrying chorus of chattering calls, before getting up to join others in fantastic aerial manoeuvres. These are among Europe' most impressive bird spectacles. They finally dive or funnel down into a reed bed, or dense forest, or on to some great building or structure such as a bridge or pi where they spend the night. Many once-famous city centre roosts have dwindled almost to nothing recentl

A spring Starling is glossy, almost unspotted, but smaller and shorter-tailed than a Blackbird, with shar more triangular wings and spiky throat feathers. Wint birds are heavily spotted with white and the wing feat have pale edging. In summer, juveniles look dull brow over, but later gain black body feathers with bold, rou white spots, contrasting with their faded brown heads Their sharp beaks, dark eye patches, waddling gait an short, square tails help separate them from other smal dark birds such as thrushes and female Blackbirds.

Starling

Sparrow

Much of C and W Europe, all year.

Winter adult

m. 75-90g.
see Blackbird, page 326.

House Sparrow

Passer domesticus

Sparrows have long been busy, noisy, social birds abo
houses and gardens, farms and town parks, more clos
associated with people than any other bird. They wer
ignored, or even disliked: people thought them coarse
unkempt, unmusical little birds. Now, as they suffer a
catastrophic decline in many areas, many realize that
they liked them after all, and miss the little sparrow i
the hedge, its rough-and-tumble existence and occasio
punch-ups.

In some places, sparrow numbers are as high as ever
but in others they have simply gone. Colonies dwindle
a year or two, reach a point at which they seem unable
function, and are snuffed out. Why this should be is a
mystery, but there are several clues. Sparrow chicks ne
insect food – caterpillars, aphids and the like – to thriv
and gardens are often devoid of such food. In winter, t
also need seeds, enough to eat all day, every day. Plant
that produce them are not necessarily abundant, sometim
completely lacking. And they need hidden, sheltered
cavities to nest in – modern buildings and improvemer
to eaves, guttering and tiles keep them firmly out.

Male House Sparrows are easily identified, with the
grey crowns, black bibs and unmarked under sides.
Females are duller, unstreaked beneath, with a broad,
pale yellow-buff stripe over each eye.

House Sparrow

Tree Sparrow

Almost everywhere,
all year.

Female

n. 25-30 g.
see Tree Sparrow, page 416.

Tree Sparrow
Passer montanus

Tree Sparrow

House Sparrow

Most of Europe, except S Spain, N Scandinavia.

Most people know a House Sparrow when they see o
but if it perches in a tree, is it or is it not a Tree Sparr
The presence of a tree has little to do with it. Tree
Sparrows of both sexes look much like male House
Sparrows: quite bright brown, streaked with black on
top, and clear buff-grey beneath. They have a similar,
often smaller, black bib, but the top of the head – wit
grey central band on the House Sparrow – is all brow
the neck has a distinct white collar and, most obvious
white cheek is marked with a square or hook of black

Tree Sparrows used to be widespread in mixed
farmland, with old trees, and near villages with holes
stone walls or old buildings. Now they are scarce, of
found quite close to water, if not exactly on the wate
edge. Maybe water encourages the insects they need
summer. In winter, they need seed, too.

You might pick up a Tree Sparrow if you know the
they chirrup and cheep like any sparrow, but have a m
distinctive note in flight, a hard, abrupt *chek*. True, it
not sound much, but if you can once link the bird and
in your mind, then you will probably recognize it aga

Juvenile

. 20-25 g.
ee House Sparrow, page 414.

Chaffinch

Fringilla coelebs

Chaffinch

Sparrow

All year in C
Europe, summer
only in N.

Park a car near a woodland picnic site and, chances a
you will be accosted by a Chaffinch or two, looking
crumbs. Their friendly approach is familiar in such
places, yet in many farmed areas they have become
rather sparse, for want of summer insects (especially
caterpillars for their chicks), and winter seed.

Chaffinches need trees and open woodland, or
woodland edges. They also freqent tall trees in bushy
hedgerows. They are at home in parks and gardens, s
long as there are trees, and come to bird tables in wi
often feeding on the ground below on seed spilled by
other birds.

In spring, the male's brown feather tips, in some
unexplained way, crumble away at the right time,
revealing brighter colours beneath. His cap turns blu
his underside salmon-pink, and the bill has a steely-b
polish. At its best, the male Chaffinch is a very smart
bird, but the female remains rather dull and olive. A
Chaffinches, though, have white on the tail and two
broad white bands across each wing, separating them
from run of the mill sparrows and other finches.

The song of a Chaffinch is a simple but cheery ph
like a musical metallic rattle with a flourish at the er
Calls are varied and apt to confuse, but a loud *pink*
is typical.

Female

Male

Female

Male

cm. 19-23 g.
ee Brambling, page 420.

Brambling

Sparrow

In winter, all of S
and W Europe.

Brambling

Fringilla montifringilla

Some of the largest flocks of birds ever seen in Europe
have been of Bramblings – ten or 11 million strong –
most people do not know what a Brambling is. These
huge flocks, typical of Central Europe, are often
Bramblings going to roost, in areas where there has been
an exceptionally abundant crop of beech mast, probably
after an unusually successful breeding season.

Bramblings breed in northern birch woods and forest
clearings, but move south and west in winter in search of
seeds. In some years, they move farther or in greater
numbers than others: in Britain, there are always
Bramblings in winter, but some years are markedly better
than most.

They join Chaffinches and Great Tits to feed under
beeches, but a few look for spilled seed under bird tables
and many feed on fields, although (in common with other
finches and buntings) they have declined on farmland as
weed seeds have diminished.

The Brambling is very like a Chaffinch, but has an
orange or yellowish chest against a white belly, and an
orange or buff upper wing bar instead of a white one. In
flight, the white rump is obvious. In winter, the bill is
yellow, unlike any Chaffinch's, but in spring it turns
shiny black, as does the male's head.

Female

Male in flight

. 22-30 g.
ee Chaffinch, page 418.

Serin

Serinus serinus

Warm spring sunshine brings the promise of a hot, d
summer across Southern Europe and the Serins are
singing: bright, tuneless, splintering twitters of sound
given from perches at the tops of trees, or by birds in
low, fast song flights on fluttering wings over fields
bright with poppies.

Serins are typically Mediterranean birds, but in
summer small numbers spread right through Central
Europe to the Baltic. They go well with bright light
sunshine: males have yellow on the forehead, under
and rump, while females are greener and more dense
streaked. A short, pale wing bar, yellow rump and d
tail help to separate them from much bigger Greenfi
and the more contrasted Siskin.

They like villages and farmsteads where all kinds
weedy growth offer an abundance of small, soft seed
and minute insects in summer. They are often aroun
olive groves and orchards, and in the open, airy cor
woods of Iberia.

Occasionally a male turns up out of range in sprin
in southern England, and sings for a while, but so far
visits have not resulted in colonisation. Autumn migra
appear, too, on headlands and islands, but these tend
dull, brown young birds and have to be distinguished
'escapes' from aviaries, such as canaries.

Serin

Sparrow

C Europe in summer.

Male

Female

n. 10-11 g.
see Siskin, Greenfinch, pages 428 and 424.

Greenfinch

Carduelis chloris

A dark patch between each small eye and a heavy, pa
pinkish beak give the Greenfinch a slightly grumpy,
frowning expression. It can look a little anonymous c
nondescript, just a dull brownish-olive bird, but whe
flies it gives itself away by flashes of lemon yellow or
edges of the wing and tail. Only by measuring the wi
of these yellow streaks can you confidently tell a brig
female from a dull male. In spring, however, both sex
become brighter and greener and the best males turn
beautifully apple-green, with striking yellow patches.

In southern Europe, Greenfinches are greener still,
look remarkably handsome in the summer sun agains
the fluttering foliage of poplars or orchard blossom.
They have simple songs, based on various ringing tri
and rattles, but some phrases are surprisingly rich an
musical. It is well worth listening to a Greenfinch in
song: it often sings from a tree top and, when the bir
can no longer contain itself, from a high, bat-like sor
flight on outstretched wings.

Greenfinches are woodland birds that flock togethe
the fields in winter, feeding on seeds. Where intensive
agriculture has made these scarce, so too are the finch
but Greenfinches also come to gardens for berries and
free helpings of peanuts and sunflower seeds if on off

Greenfinch

Sparrow

Except far north,
all year.

Female

Spring male

n. 25-30 g.
see House Sparrow, Siskin, pages 414 and 428.

Goldfinch

Carduelis carduelis

Where the willows thin out at the rough edge of a gra
pit and open ground takes over, with bramble brakes
a scattering of tall sowthistles, and where summer spi
of teazels produce a profusion of tough, spiny, lilac
blooms – this is the place for Goldfinches. They are s
and delicate, with long bills for probing into bristly
flower heads for soft, half-ripe seeds. Their speciality
feeding on tall weedy plants in unkempt places, gathe
on the thistles that persist, despite efforts to rid them
from the pastures. In winter, they join Siskins and
Redpolls in the search for alder seeds.

Goldfinches rarely make large flocks in such places
but sometimes in a cornfield in the south you might s
hundred or two together, a memorable sight. They are
easy to identify, with their soft, lisping, *swilt-swilt-sw*
calls, bouncy flight, red, white and black faces and br
bands of yellow across black wings. They make you
wonder why so many birds have to be streaky brown
when this one can survive well enough in such an
extravagance of colour. Young ones have the same wi
pattern, although the yellow is less brilliant and the b
dull, each feather with a buff tip. They have a plain,
greyish head for some weeks, but there is never any
doubt that they are Goldfinches.

Goldfinch

Sparrow

Not Scandinavia.
All year.

Immature

Adult

m. 14-17 g.
see Siskin, Linnet, pages 428 and 430.

Siskin
Carduelis spinus

Few European birds are smaller than the Siskin: for a finch, it is tiny and finely built, with a sharp, triangul beak made for probing for seeds in the cones of larch and alders. It has adapted this feeding method to take peanuts from hanging baskets, too, especially in sprir when natural foods are in short supply. Many people only see Siskins in their gardens, but bigger numbers usually found in and around conifer plantations, or in the trees along lowland streams.

When they fly, Siskin flocks have a more co-ordina look than those of most larger finches, sweeping out long, open arcs before returning to rain down into th tree once more, where they twitter loudly with a rapi undistinguished chorus and various buzzing notes. Th flight calls are much purer – beautiful and far-carryin notes, with a slightly metallic, squeaky quality, somet like *tsy-zu* or *psy-eee*. Such notes form the basis of sp song, too, which is often heard in the wintering areas before the birds move north, or uphill, to breed in coniferous woods.

Males are green with dusky streaks, black and brig yellow on the wings, and a clear lime-green or yellow the breast, while females are much whiter where male are yellow. Their tiny size, narrow dark streaks and th pale wing bars help to identify them.

Siskin

Sparrow

Mostly in N and mountains.

Winter
male

Female

Juvenile

Female

n. 12-17 g.
see Greenfinch, page 424.

Linnet

Carduelis cannabina

Several small finches feed on seeds, which tend to be abundant locally, but not universally or widely spread. usual habit of selecting nesting territories, which sprea birds evenly over the landscape, does not work for Linnets. Instead, they breed in small, loose colonies, a can feed amicably together where their food is availab

The Linnet is a small, colourful finch of heaths, farmland hedgerows and the lower slopes of upland moors. In Southern Europe, it is found in similar situations, but much higher on the hills. In winter, Linnets form bigger flocks, dancing over the fields in bounding, twittering flights between bouts of feeding the ground. They are neither agile nor light enough t acrobatic on tall plant stems or slender twigs.

The white wing and tail flashes are useful, but not conclusive identification marks. In summer, the fema much the same as in winter, ginger-brown and buff, with a greyer head, a pale cheek spot and short, blac legs, and the same flash of white on the side of each wing and the tail. The male, whose wings are more b and white, develops a beautiful flush of crimson on t head and breast, and sits on bush tops to sing, with a sophisticated, musical sequence of warbles, trills ar twittering call notes. If any bird twitters, it's the Lin

Linnet

Sparrow

Most of Europe. N
birds move S and
W in winter.

Spring male

Female

. 14-20 g.
ee Twite, page 432.

Twite

Carduelis flavirostris

Of all the finches, the Twite is the most dependent on
seeds: it even feeds its chicks on small seeds, while ot
feed them on nutritious caterpillars. This is the Twite
undoing in many areas, as herbicides have reduced th
common weeds around field edges that have, for
centuries, produced the bird's year-round food. The
ancestral Twite habitats are small hay meadows and
weedy fringes of pastures in the uplands, or around
western coasts and islands, often in little isolated
depressions between rocky hills. Such places have
remained unchanged for long periods but now, with
more efficient agriculture, they offer fewer opportun
for this neat little finch.

In winter, Twites move to lower ground, especially
edges of coastal salt marshes and muddy estuaries. T
behave much like Linnets, feeding inconspicuously in
flocks on the ground among low vegetation and
periodically flying up briefly to swirl around, calling
then drop down again in sudden silence. The white
streaks on wing and tail look much like a Linnet's, b
the streaky, tawny body and buff wing bar remind o
a Redpoll. The clear, orange-buff throat is distinctive
is the yellow bill in winter. The call is a nasal, twang
twai-it or *dwee-it*, interspersed with a hard, metallic
chatter, which also forms the basis of the song.

Twite

Sparrow

Mainly in N. Moves
to coasts in winter.

. 13-19 g.
ee Linnet, Redpoll, pages 430 and 434.

Common & Lesser Redpol

Carduelis flammea and *Carduelis cab*

Redpolls are often thought of in association with Sis
and they are frequently found together in mixed floc
They are almost as small, and equally tiny-billed as
Siskins, but a little more elongated and long in the ta
Like Siskins, they are remarkably acrobatic feeders,
in the tiniest twiglets of birch and larch.

Most look dull, pale brownish, whiter below, with
tiny black chin, a dark red cap that is not easy to see
and a prominent bar of tawny-buff across each wing
spring, males become brighter, flushed with a lovely
pink on the breast: some are very vivid. In Britain, tl
redpolls are browner and smaller than on the Europe
mainland, and are described as **Lesser Redpolls,** a
separate species. However, winter flocks may include
larger, paler birds, with whiter wing bars, that are
characteristic of northern Europe, and known as
Common Redpolls (or to some by their former name
Mealy Redpolls). Again, these have been classified a
separate species in their own right. The closely relate
Arctic Redpolls are bigger, brighter, white on the rur
and with even tinier beaks.

A singing redpoll bounds across the birch trees,
hawthorn bushes and small conifers of its breeding
habitat with harsh, metallic rattling notes intersperse
with a fast, vibrating trill. This last is its simple song

Common Redpoll

Sparrow

Much of Europe, all
year in N and W.

Female
Common
Redpoll, winter

Male Common
Redpoll, winter

Male Lesser
Redpoll

_esser
winter

Lesser Redpoll

Sparrow

Britain, N and C
Europe.

non: 12 cm. 10-12 g.
: 12 cm. 12 g.
ee Twite, Siskin, pages 432 and 428.

Common Crossbill

Loxia curvirostra

This small bird, with its peculiarly cross-tipped bill th[...]
has evolved to prise open pine cones, ought to be a
simple matter. But crossbills are an extraordinarily
complex subject. It has long been known that there is
bigger northern species, the Parrot Crossbill, and the
Crossbills of the old pine forests of Scotland have bee[...]
separated as another, intermediate, species. Then ther[...]
are, apparently, various forms of crossbill across Euro[...]
looking or sounding a little different from each other
Recently it has been shown that these nomadic group[...]
turning up in various areas in some years but not oth[...]
have consistently different calls. Something keeps the[...]
apart genetically, so are they, too, separate micro-spe[...]

All crossbills are chunky, long-winged finches, fee[...]
on seeds of conifers. Pine-seed eaters have massively
broad, heavy bills, while those of larch-seed feeders a[...]
smaller. In most, the adult males are bright red and t[...]
females greenish, with yellow or orange rumps. Thei[...]
calls, varied as they are, have a common loud, stacca[...]
ringing quality that echoes around the woods. These
startling *chip-chip-chip* calls are the usual clues to th[...]
presence. When they feed, usually hidden in the coni[...]
tops, they are quiet, apart from the cracking of seed[...]
the quiet tapping of falling litter from the split cones[...]

Crossbill

Sparrow

Scattered widely in
late summer, autumn.

Old male

Young male

Juvenile

Female

n. 35-50 g.
see Greenfinch, page 424.

Pine Grosbeak & Common Rosefinc

Pinicola enucleator and
Carpodacus eruthrinus

These chunky finches were both called grosbeaks unti recent changes in classification. The name fits the hea bill perfectly. The **Common Rosefinch** used also to be called the Scarlet Rosefinch, but scarlet only describes the summer male, which boasts a beautiful strawberr red on the head and fore parts. Young ones and fema are rather dull olive-brown, with thin, pale wing bars soft streaks and dark button-eyes set in plain, round heads. They can be puzzling birds when encountered unexpectedly, but the bulbous bill helps to separate th from other finches. They are quite widespread in Northern and north-eastern Europe, but rare migrant Britain, hardly known away from the coast. Most of those seen are dull autumn juveniles.

Pine Grosbeaks are much bigger, hefty birds, like o sized Bullfinches, but more acrobatic when feeding, almost parrot-like while contriving to reach the last, juiciest, berry. They breed far to the north and hardly migrate, but may move a little south in winter, or penetrate more urban areas. There, like Waxwings, th can be remarkably oblivious to the presence of people All have white under the tail, often obvious as they ti over to feed, they also have two long, white wing bar Males are raspberry-red and females yellow-olive wit bronze cast, both often with much pale grey mixed in

Pine Grosbeak

Sparrow

N and NE, moving
S in winter.

Female

Female Pine Grosbeak

e Grosbeak

le
non Rosefinch

Male
Common
Rosefinch

Grosbeak: 20 cm. 50-60 g. Also see Crossbill, page 436.
non Rosefinch: 14 cm. 19-25 g. Also see Linnet, Redpoll,
s 430 and 434.

Common Rosefinch

Sparrow

N and E, summer.

Bullfinch

Pyrrhula pyrrhula

For reasons that are not entirely clear, this bird is in dec
across Europe, which is a great shame. Formerly consid
a pest in fruit growing areas, when numbers were high,
a truly beautiful bird and a chance encounter is now a
memorable occasion.

Bullfinches are bull-necked, with short, very broad, c
and rounded bills. The bill is not a great seed-cracker, b
manipulator of soft buds and fruits, the seeds of ash ke
and half-formed, semi-ripe seeds of various shrubs and
trees. This is the Bullfinch's special role in life, and its
efficiency at stripping fruit trees infuriated many a gard
before its numbers declined.

A Bullfinch typically slips off if disturbed, diving qui
through a hedge, but it is given away by its broad, strik
white rump, that marks its route, until it disappears. A
female is warm brown, with blacker wings and a black
cap; the juvenile is similar, but without the black cap. A
male, however, is wonderfully rose-red below, pale grey
above, with blue-black wings crossed by a band of dull
white, a black cap and a small black chin. It is hardly t
confused with anything else: no Chaffinch has a black
or white rump, and nothing is so brightly red-pink in fr

The Bullfinch almost lacks an obvious song: it make
quiet, creaky pea-whistle sounds. Its call, however, is
distinctive: a low, pure, fluty whistle on one note.

Bullfinch

Sparrow

Most of Europe,
all year.

Male

Female

m. 20-25 g.
see Chaffinch, page 418.

Hawfinch

Sparrow

Most of Europe,
all year.

Hawfinch

Coccothraustes coccothraustes

Hawfinches, always scarce, have now become rarities
almost everywhere. It is a treat to see one, a real find
you come across it by chance, and difficult to get to
grips with even if you learn of a likely location. Such
places are fairly well known, as Hawfinches remain
faithful to traditional areas, often hillside woods, or
big, well-wooded parks. They like mature trees, beech,
oak, and very often lofty limes, together with wild
cherry and hornbeam.

Such places are not so scarce, but few satisfy this shy
and elusive finch, with its bull-neck, large head and
heavy bill, recalling the silhouette of a Crossbill. When
you do see one, it is surprisingly often a good view and
close scrutiny reveals peculiar, bill-hook-shaped feathers
on the wing. Overall, it is tawny-coloured, with a splash
of dull white across the wing and a white tip to the tail;
in flight, the wide white wing bars are more striking.

Two or three, or half a dozen, will feed together on
the ground, or fly up to the very tops of the trees. They
sit still and look about for minutes on end, now and
then making a remarkably Robin-like, sharp *tick* – an
insignificant noise, but worth learning if you wish to
see a Hawfinch.

n. 25-30 g.
see Chaffinch, page 418.

Lapland Bunting

Calcarius lapponicus

On the high, central spine of Norway and Sweden, a
on the far northern tundra, Lapland Buntings can be
in their breeding colours, but for most Europeans, if
are seen at all, they are winter birds.

In Britain, it is a scarce autumn and winter migran
unknown to the majority, except for a few birdwatch
who look for them on saltmarshes and coastal fields
dotted about the east coast, or on headlands and isla
in autumn. They are inconspicuous, keeping to the
ground, even out of sight in rank grass, or shuffling
about on more open ground with stones and rocks. T
female looks a little like a female Reed Bunting, but i
low-slung bird, with a longer bodied, shorter-tailed e
and short, dark legs. Useful clues are a band of rusty
edged with fine buff lines, across the middle of the w
a pale central line on the top of the head, and little d
triangles at each corner of the cheeks.

The winter male is more strikingly marked, with a
of summer colour: a yellow bill, a broad rusty patch
the back of the neck and variable blackish streaks on
throat and chest. A short, hard, rattled call is anothe
helpful feature.

Lapland Bunting

Sparrow

Scandinavia, summer,
NW European coasts
in winter.

Male, summer

Female, autumn

Male, spring

Female, autumn

n. 25-28 g.
see Reed Bunting, page 452.

Snow Bunting
Plectrophenax nivalis

Snow Bunting

Sparrow

Mainly seen winter.

In summer, Snow Buntings are confined to a few peaks
Scotland, the high spine and coasts of northern
Scandinavia, and Iceland. Few people see these black a
white birds of the breeding season. In autumn, they m
south and to lower levels, but everywhere they are loc:
and scarce.

This is not a bird that you come across by chance: yo
need to go and see it. Its typical location is a broad, san
beach in winter backed by dunes and some saltmarsh w
bare patches swept by the highest tides, plus a shingle
ridge. Here you have a chance of seeing a small flock o
Snow Buntings wandering widely around these habitats
sometimes elusive, sometimes remarkably confiding.

They creep about on short, black legs, looking long, l
slung, tapered and almost lark-like, but with round heac
and thick, yellow bills. They are more richly coloured th
most people expect: much of the white, even on largely
white-winged adult males, is hidden and they look buff,
brown and black, with tawny-red on the face and chest
flight they suddenly reveal white wings with bars and
patches, the amount of white varying according to age :
sex. The flock flies off with a flickering effect, a flurry c
snowflakes, and a burst of rippling calls, before droppi
to the ground and 'disappearing' again amongst the
colourful textures of shingle and beach vegetation.

Female or juvenile

n summer

Males in winter

n. 30-35 g.
see Lapland Bunting, page 444.

Yellowhamme

Emberiza citrinella

Yellowhammer

Sparrow

Most of Europe, all year. Moves S in winter.

Untidy farmsteads in upland fields where there are st
some hedges, a scattering of cattle and perhaps spille
seed and straw, attract small groups of Yellowhamme
in winter. Stubble fields used to, but are now rare. Th
Yellowhammers get up as you approach with a
distinctive, sharp, metallic *tswik*! and fly for cover in
nearest hedge.

If it is summer, head for a heath, or the lower brac
covered slopes of moorland, or a long, low hedgerow
undulating farmland, or perhaps some rough grassy
slopes with scattered hawthorns and bramble patches
the coast: in any or all of these you should find some
Yellowhammers. They sing all day, all summer long: .
simple repetition of a sharp note, followed by one or
longer, higher, or lower, ones – *ti-ti-ti-ti-ti-ti-ti-teeee-t*
Such is the best of the commoner bunting songs, but
effect is pleasant enough, especially when given by a
beautiful little bird clothed in rusty-brown, black and
clear, if rather flat, lemon-yellow.

The female is browner, but still distinctive enough,
with rusty-red or ginger rump, a black and white tail
at least a hint of yellow on the face and breast: enoug
to separate it at least from most common heath or
farmland birds.

Male

Female

Female

. 25-30 g.
ee Cirl Bunting, page 450.

Cirl Bunting

Emberiza cirlus

In Southern Europe, wherever there are warm slopes, sunny fields and bushy places with scattered trees, you will hear the simple, jingling phrases of singing Cirl Buntings. They make a metallic trill, a little like a Yellowhammer without its long '*cheese*', or a faster, dribbling trill with an even speed and pitch. The song a Bonelli's Warbler is similar, but a little looser, more a bubble than a trill: you will need to make your own comparisons. However you think of it, Cirl Bunting s is characteristic of a Mediterranean spring, as is the much more elusive quiet, sharp *stip* call.

In England, Cirl Buntings used to be widespread, e quite common, but have now almost disappeared: th are confined to Devon, with a 'new' population reloc to Cornwall. They need bushy hedges beside old past and a reliable supply of grasshoppers, for their chick

A female Cirl Bunting is a tricky bird to identify: i like a female Yellowhammer with a frowning express and a dull rump (instead of rufous). A male, howeve a fine and distinctive bird, a 'hard' shade of rusty-red above, streaked with black, yellowish below with rus flanks and a greenish breast band and boldly pattern with yellow and black on the head. The black throat especially eyecatching and diagnostic.

Cirl Bunting

Sparrow

Mainly S Europe.

Male

Female

25 g.
e Yellowhammer, page 448.

Reed Bunting
Emberiza schoeniclus

Take a walk in spring: head downhill, for you need t
find a wet place, a marshy spot or a dense growth of
sedges, reedmace and reed around a lake or flooded
or in a low-lying, untidy riverside meadow. Short gra
by a cycle path beside a reservoir won't do: the
vegetation has to be taller, ideally rough and irregula

Listen for a short, jangling, unmusical song, little
than four or five notes strung together with no real
pattern, repeated with monotonous regularity. Look
the singer – one could almost say the culprit, the so
so undistinguished – on an upright stem. There you
your Reed Bunting.

What it lacks in musical virtuosity the male make
for in appearance, for this is a smart, slender, long-ta
bird, streaked sandy-brown, black and cream to go
the dead grasses and reeds, with bold white sides to
black tail, and best of all a black hood above a broa
collar of white. The female is trickier, having the
distinctive tail and similar contrasting streaks, but a
much weaker pattern of cream, pale brown and rust
iron colour on the head. Something about the beak,
curve of the smaller upper mandible against the larg
lower one, also suggests this is a bunting, not a finc

Reed Bunting

Sparrow

In winter, leaves N
and E.

Summer male

Female

Winter male

, 16-20 g.
ee Corn Bunting, page 454.

Corn Bunting

Miliaria calandra

Most buntings make up for their lack of a fine song colourful plumage. The Corn Bunting struggles, bei pale brown and cream with black streaks. It doesn't have the white sides to the tail that are typical of buntings: its long tail is just brown, like the rest of

Yet, it is a smart little bird if you see it closely, an look at it in the right way, to appreciate the delicate touches and neatness of its streaks and stripes. Like bird, it has its own appeal. It is bigger than other buntings, most finches and sparrows, more like a b lark, but compared with the Skylark – which does h white on the tail – it has a heavier, more triangular and a rounder head, and it is likely to sit on a high

In much of Britain and Western Europe, the Corn Bunting has withdrawn into small pockets where it remains frequent. In Southern Europe, however, it i common in farmland and bushy places. Its song is everywhere: a dry jingling, like a brief shake of a b of keys, or the tinkle of falling shards of glass. Not musical masterpiece, but like many others, it is just for its environment, like the shrill of a grasshopper heat of a summer day in a dry, grassy meadow.

Corn Bunting

Sparrow

Most of Europe,
all year.

m. 40-50 g.
see Skylark, page 282.

A

Accipiter gentilis, Goshawk, 126

Accipiter nisus, Sparrowhawk, 128

Acrocephalus schoenobaenus, Sedge
   Warbler, 340

Acrocephalus scirpaceus, Reed
   Warbler, 342

Aegithalos caudatus, Long-tailed Tit,
   372

Alauda arvensis, Sand Martin, 284

Alauda arvensis, Skylark, 282

Alca torda, Razorbill, 226

Alcedo atthis, Kingfisher, 260

Alectoris rufa, Red-legged Partridge,
   72

Anas acuta, Pintail, 40

Anas clypeata, Shoveler, 44

Anas crecca, Teal, 36

Anas penelope, Wigeon, 32

Anas platyrhynchos, Mallard, 38

Anas querquedula, Garganey, 42

Anas strepera, Gadwall, 34

Anser albifrons, White-fronted Goose,
   20

Anser anser, Greylag Goose, 22

Anser brachyrhynchus, Pink-footed
   Goose, 18

Anser fabalis, Bean Goose, 16

Anthus petrosus, Rock Pipit, 294

Anthus pratensis, Meadow Pipit, 292

Anthus spinoletta, Water Pipit, 294

Anthus trivialis, Tree Pipit, 292

Apus apus, Swift, 256

Apus melba, Alpine Swift, 258

Aquila chryseatos, Golden Eagle, 134

Arctitis hypoleucos, Common
   Sandpiper, 198

Ardea cinerea, Grey Heron, 104

Arenaria interpres, Turnstone, 200

Asio flammeus, Short-eared Owl, 248

Asio otus, Long-eared Owl, 24

Athene noctua, Little Owl, 24

Avocet, *Recurvirostra avosetta*,

Aythea ferina, Pochard, 46

Aythya fuligula, Tufted Duck,

Aythya marila, Scaup, 50

B

Bee-eater, *Merops apiaster*, 26.

Bittern, *Botaurus stellaris*, 100

Blackbird, *Turdus merula*, 326

Blackcap, *Sylvia atricapilla*, 35

Bluethroat, *Luscinia svecica*, 3

Bombycilla garrulus, Waxwing

Botaurus stellaris, Bittern, 100

Brambling, *Fringilla montifrin*
   420

Branta bernicla, Brent Goose,

Branta canadensis, Canada Go

Branta leucopsis, Barnacle Goo

Bubo bubo, Eagle Owl, 250

Bucephala clangula, Goldeney

Bullfinch, *Pyrrhula pyrrhula*, 4

Bunting, Cirl, *Emberiza cirlus*,

Bunting, Corn, *Miliaria calana*

Bunting, Lapland, *Calcarius
   lapponicus*, 444

Bunting, Reed, *Emberiza scho*
   452

Bunting, Snow, *Plectrophenax*
   446

Burhinus oedicnemus, Stone-c
   160

Buteo buteo, Buzzard, 130

Buteo lagopus, Rough-legged
   Buzzard, 132

Buzzard, *Buteo buteo*, 130

Buzzard, Honey, *Pernis apivor*

Buzzard, Rough-legged, *Buteo
   lagopus*, 132

arius lapponicus, Lapland
   unting, 444
Iris alba, Sanderling, 174
Iris alpina, Dunlin, 180
Iris canutus, Knot, 172
Iris ferruginea, Curlew Sandpiper,
   76
Iris maritima, Purple Sandpiper,
   78
Iris minuta, Little Stint, 176
rcaillie, Tetrao urogallus, 70
imulgus europeaus, Nightjar, 254
uelis cabaret, Lesser Redpoll, 434
uelis carduelis, Goldfinch, 426
uelis chloris, Greenfinch, 424
uelis flammea, Common Redpoll,
   ·4
uelis flavirostris, Twite, 432
uelis spinus, Siskin, 428
uleis cannabina, Linnet, 430
odacus erythrinus, Common
   osefinch, 438
hus grylle, Black Guillemot, 228
ia brachydactyla, Short-toed
   eecreeper, 388
ia familiaris, Treecreeper, 388
cetti, Cetti's Warbler, 336
inch, Frigilla coelebs, 418
drius dubia, Little Ringed
   over, 162
drius hiaticula, Ringed Plover,
   4
onias niger, Black Tern, 224
haff, Phylloscopus collybita,
   3
h, Pyrrhocorax pyrrhocorax,
   2
a ciconia, White Stork, 106
s cinclus, Dipper, 304

Circus aeruginosus, Marsh Harrier,
   120
Circus cyaneus, Hen Harrier, 122
Circus pygargus, Montagu's Harrier,
   124
Clangula hyemalis, Long-tailed Duck,
   54
Coccothraustes coccothraustes,
   Hawfinch, 442
Columba livia, Rock Dove, 230
Columba oenas, Stock Dove, 232
Columba palumbus, Wood Pigeon,
   234
Coot, *Fulica atra,* 150
Cormorant, *Phalacrocorax carbo,* 96
Corncrake, *Crex crex,* 74
Corvus corax, Raven, 410
Corvus corone, Carrion
   Crow/Hooded Crow, 408
Corvus frugilegus, Rook, 406
Corvus monedula, Jackdaw, 404
Coturnix coturnix, Quail, 74
Crane, *Grus grus,* 152
Crex crex, Corncrake, 74
Crossbill, *Loxia curvirostra,* 436
Crow, Carrion/Hooded, *Corvus
   corone,* 408
Cuckoo, *Cuculus canorus,* 240
Cuculus canorus, Cuckoo, 240
Curlew, *Numenius arquata,* 190
Cygnus colombianus, Bewick's Swan,
   14
Cygnus cygnus, Whooper Swan, 14
Cygnus olor, Mute Swan, 12

D

Delichon urbica, House Martin, 290
Dendrocopos minor, Lesser Spotted
   Woodpecker, 276
Dipper, *Cinclus cinclus,* 304

Diver, Black-throated, *Gavia arctica*, 78

Diver, Great Northern, *Gavia immer*, 80

Diver, Red-throated, *Gavia stellata*, 78

Dove, Collared, *Streptopelia decaocto*, 236

Dove, Rock, *Columba livia*, 230

Dove, Stock, *Columba oenas*, 232

Dove, Turtle, *Streptopelia turtur*, 238

Dryocopus martius, Black Woodpecker, 272

Dendrocopos major, Great Spotted Woodpecker, 274

Duck, Long-tailed, *Clangula hyemalis*, 54

Duck, Tufted, *Aythya fuligula*, 48

Dunlin, *Calidris alpina*, 180

Dunnock, *Prunella modularis*, 308

E

Eagle, Golden, *Aquila chryseatos*, 134

Eagle, White-tailed, *Haliaeetus albicilla*, 116

Egret, Little, *Egretta garzetta*, 102

Egretta garzetta, Little Egret, 102

Eider, *Somateria mollissima*, 52

Emberiza cirlus, Cirl Bunting, 450

Emberiza citrinella, Yellowhammer, 448

Emberiza schoeniclus, Reed Bunting, 452

Erithacus rubecula, Robin, 310

F

Falco columbarius, Merlin, 140

Falco peregrinus, Peregrine, 144

Falco subbuteo, Hobby, 142

Falco tinnunculus, Kestrel, 138

Ficedula hypoleuca, Pied Flycatc 368

Fieldfare, *Turdus pilaris*, 328

Firecrest, *Regulus ignicapillus*, 3

Flycatcher, Pied, *Ficedula hypol* 368

Flycatcher, Spotted, *Muscicapa* 366

Fratercula arctica, Puffin, 228

Frigilla coelebs, Chaffinch, 418

Fringilla montifringilla, Brambl 420

Fulica atra, Coot, 150

Fulmar, *Fumarus glacialis*, 90

Fumarus glacialis, Fulmar, 90

G

Gadwall, *Anas strepera*, 34

Galerida cristata, Crested Lark 278

Galiniago gallinago, Snipe, 184

Gallinula chloropus, Moorhen,

Gannet, *Morus bassanus*, 94

Garganey, *Anas querquedula*, 4

Garrulus glandarius, Jay, 396

Gavia arctica, Black-throated I 78

Gavia immer, Great Northern 80

Gavia stellata, Red-throated D

Glaucidium passerinum, Pygm 252

Godwit, Bar-tailed, *Limosa lap* 188

Godwit, Black-tailed, *Limosa* 188

Goldcrest, *Regulus regulus*, 36

Goldeneye, *Bucephala clangul*

Goldfinch, *Carduelis carduelis*

Goosander, *Mergus merganser*

e, Barnacle, *Branta leucopsis*, 26
e, Bean, *Anser fabalis*, 16
e, Brent, *Branta bernicla*, 28
e, Canada, *Branta canadensis*, 24
e, Greylag, *Anser anser*, 22
e, Pink-footed, *Anser achyrhynchus*, 18
e, White-fronted, *Anser bifrons*, 20
awk, *Accipiter gentilis*, 126
e, Black-necked, *Podiceps gricollis*, 88
e, Great Crested, *Podiceps istatus*, 84
e, Little, *Tachybaptus ruficollis*,

e, Red-necked, *Podiceps isegena*, 86
e, Slavonian, *Podiceps auritus*, 88
finch, *Carduelis chloris*, 424
shank, *Tringa nebularia*, 194
peak, Pine, *Pinicola enucleator*, 8
se, Black, *Tetrao tetrix*, 68
se, Red/Willow, *Lagopus gopus*, 66
grus, Crane, 152
emot, *Uria aalge*, 226
emot, Black, *Cepphus grylle*, 228
Black-headed, *Larus ridibundus*, 8
Common, *Larus canus*, 210
Great Black-backed, *Larus arinus*, 216
Herring, *Larus argentatus*, 214
Lesser Black-backed, *Larus scus*, 212
Little, *Larus minutus*, 206
Mediterranean, *Larus elanocephalus*, 206

Gull, Yellow-legged, *Larus cachinnans*, 214
Gyps fulvus, Griffon Vulture, 118

H
Haematopus ostralegus, Oystercatcher, 154
Haliaeetus albicilla, White-tailed Eagle, 116
Harrier, Hen, *Circus cyaneus*, 122
Harrier, Marsh, *Circus aeruginosus*, 120
Harrier, Montagu's, *Circus pygargus*, 124
Hawfinch, *Coccothraustes coccothraustes*, 442
Heron, Grey, *Ardea cinerea*, 104
Himantopus himantopus, Black-winged Stilt, 156
Hippolais icterina, Icterine Warbler, 344
Hippolais polyglotta, Melodius Warbler, 344
Hirundo rupestris, Crag Martin, 286
Hirundo rustica, Swallow, 288
Hobby, *Falco subbuteo*, 142
Hoopoe, *Upupa epops*, 264

J
Jackdaw, *Corvus monedula*, 404
Jay, *Garrulus glandarius*, 396
Jay, Siberian, *Perisorius infaustus*, 398
Jynx torquilla, Wryneck, 266

K
Kestrel, *Falco tinnunculus*, 138
Kingfisher, *Alcedo atthis*, 260
Kite, Black, *Milvus migrans*, 112
Kite, Red, *Milvus milvus*, 114
Kittiwake, *Rissa Tridactyla*, 218
Knot, *Calidris canutus*, 172

L

Lagopus lagopus, Red Grouse/Willow
  Grouse, 66
Lanius collurio, Red-backed Shrike,
  392
Lanius excubitor, Great Grey Shrike,
  394
Lapwing, *Vanellus vanellus,* 170
Lark, Crested, *Galerida cristata,*
  278
Larus argentatus, Herring Gull, 214
Larus cachinnans, Yellow-legged Gull,
  214
Larus canus, Common Gull, 210
Larus fuscus, Lesser Black-backed
  Gull, 212
Larus Marinus, Great Black-backed
  Gull, 216
Larus melanocephalus, Mediterranean
  Gull, 206
Larus minutus, Little Gull, 206
Larus ridibundus, Black-headed Gull,
  208
Limosa lapponica, Bar-tailed Godwit,
  188
Limosa limosa, Black-tailed Godwit,
  188
Linnet, *Carduleis cannabina,* 430
Locustella naevia, Grasshopper
  Warbler, 338
Loxia curvirostra, Crossbill, 436
Lullula arborea, Woodlark, 280
Luscinia luscinia, Thrush Nightingale,
  312
Luscinia megarhynchos, Nightingale,
  312
Luscinia svecica, Bluethroat, 314
Lymnocryptes minimus, Jack Snipe,
  184

M

Magpie, *Pica pica,* 400
Mallard, *Anas platyrhynchos,* 3
Martin, Crag, *Hirundo rupestr*
  286
Martin, House, *Delichon urbic*
Martin, Sand, *Alauda arvensis,*
Melanitta fusca, Velvet Scoter, *Melanitta nigra,* Common Scot
Merganser, Red-breasted, *Merg*
  serrator, 62
Mergus albellus, Smew, 60
Mergus merganser, Goosander,
Mergus serrator, Red-breasted
  Merganser, 62
Merlin, *Falco columbarius,* 14C
Merops apiaster, Bee-eater, 262
Miliaria calandra, Corn buntin
Milvus migrans, Black Kite, 11
Milvus milvus, Red Kite, 114
Moorhen, *Gallinula chloropus,*
Morus bassanus, Gannet, 94
Motacilla alba, Pied Wagtail, 3
Motacilla cinera, Grey Wagtail,
Motacilla flava, Yellow Wagtail
Muscicapa striata, Spotted Flyc
  366

N

Neophron percnopterus, Egypt
  Vulture, 118
Nightingale, *Luscinia megarhy*
  312
Nightingale, Thrush, *Luscinia*
  luscinia, 312
Nightjar, *Caprimulgus europae*
Nucifraga caryocatactes, Nutcr
  386
Numenius arquata, Curlew, 19
Numenius phaeopus, Whimbre

:acker, *Nucifraga caryocatactes*,
6
atch, *Sitta europaea*, 384

nthe oenanthe, Wheatear, 322
e, Golden, *Oriolus oriolus*, 390
us oriolus, Golden Oriole, 390
:y, *Pandion haliaetus*, 136
, Ring, *Turdus torquatus*, 324
Barn, *Tyto alba*, 242
Eagle, *Bubo bubo*, 250
Little, *Athene noctua*, 244
Long-eared, *Asio otus*, 248
Pygmy, *Glaucidium passerinum*,
2
Short-eared, *Asio flammeus*, 248
Tawny, *Strix aluco*, 246
:rcatcher, *Haematopus*
tralegus, 154

on haliaetus, Osprey, 136
us biarmicus, Bearded Tit, 370
lge, Grey, *Perdrix perdrix*, 72
dge, Red-legged, *Alectoris rufa*,

ater, Coal Tit, 378
caeruleus, Blue Tit, 380
cristatus, Crested Tit, 376
major, Great Tit, 382
montanus, Willow Tit, 374
palustris, Marsh Tit, 374
· *domesticus*, House Sparrow,
4

· *montanus*, Tree Sparrows, 416
ix perdrix, Grey Partridge, 72
:ine, *Falco peregrinus*, 144
rius infaustus, Siberian Jay, 398
apivorus, Honey Buzzard, 110

Phalacrocorax aristotelis, Shag, 98
Phalacrocorax carbo, Cormorant, 96
Phasianus colchicus, Pheasant, 76
Pheasant, *Phasianus colchicus*, 76
Philomachus pugnax, Ruff, 182
Phoenicurus ochruros, Black Redstart,
316
Phoenicurus phoenicurus, Redstart,
316
Phylloscopus collybita, Chiffchaff,
358
Phylloscopus sibilatrix, Wood
Warbler, 356
Phylloscopus trochilus, Willow
Warbler, 360
Pica pica, Magpie, 400
Picus canus, Grey-headed
Woodpecker, 268
Picus viridis, Green Woodpecker, 270
Pigeon, Wood, *Columba palumbus*,
234
Pinicola enucleator, Pine Grosbeak,
438
Pintail, *Anas acuta*, 40
Pipit, Meadow, *Anthus pratensis*, 292
Pipit, Rock, *Anthus petrosus*, 294
Pipit, Tree, *Anthus trivialis*, 292
Pipit, Water, *Anthus spinoletta*, 294
Platalea leucorodia, Spoonbill, 108
Plectrophenax nivalis, Snow Bunting,
446
Plover, Golden, *Pluvialis apricaria*,
166
Plover, Grey, *Pluvialis squatarola*, 168
Plover, Little Ringed, *Charadrius*
dubia, 162
Plover, Ringed, *Charadrius*
hiaticula,164
Pluvialis apricaria, Golden Plover, 166
Pluvialis squatarola, Grey Plover, 168

Pochard, *Aythea ferina*, 46

Podiceps auritus, Slavonian Grebe, 88

Podiceps cristatus, Great Crested Grebe, 84

Podiceps grisegena, Red-necked Grebe, 86

Podiceps nigricollis, Black-necked Grebe, 88

Prunella modularis, Dunnock, 308

Puffin, *Fratercula arctica,* 228

Puffinus puffinus, Manx Shearwater, 92

Pyrrhocorax pyrrhocorax, Chough, 402

Pyrrhula pyrrhula, Bullfinch, 440

Q

Quail, *Coturnix coturnix,* 74

R

Rail, Water, *Rallus aquaticus,* 146

Rallus aquaticus, Water Rail, 146

Raven, *Corvus corax,* 410

Razorbill, *Alca torda,* 226

Recurvirostra avosetta, Avocet, 158

Redpoll, Common, *Carduelis flammea,* 434

Redpoll, Lesser, *Carduelis cabaret,* 434

Redshank, *Tringa totanus,* 192

Redshank, Spotted, *Tringa erythropus,* 192

Redstart, *Phoenicurus phoenicurus,* 316

Redstart, Black, *Phoenicurus ochruros,* 316

Redwing, *Turdus iliacus,* 332

Regulus ignicapillus, Firecrest, 364

Regulus regulus, Goldcrest, 362

Remiz pendulinus, Penduline T

Rissa Tridactyla, Kittiwake, 21

Robin, *Erithacus rubecula,* 310

Rook, *Corvus frugilegus,* 406

Rosefinch, Common, *Carpoda erythrinus,* 438

Ruff, *Philomachus pugnax,* 182

S

Sanderling, *Calidris alba,* 174

Sandpiper, Common, *Arctitis hypoleucos,* 198

Sandpiper, Curlew, *Calidris ferruginea,* 176

Sandpiper, Green, *Tringa ochro* 196

Sandpiper, Purple, *Calidris mar* 178

Sandpiper, Wood, *Tringa glare* 196

Saxicola rubetra, Whinchat, 31

Saxicola torquata, Stonechat, 3

Scaup, *Aythya marila,* 50

Scolopax rusticola, Woodcock,

Scoter, Common, *Melanitta nig*

Scoter, Velvet, *Melanitta fusca,*

Serin, *Serinus serinus,* 422

Serinus serinus, Serin, 422

Shag, *Phalacrocorax aristotelis,*

Shearwater, Manx, *Puffinus pu* 92

Shelduck, *Tadorna tadorna,* 30

Shoveler, *Anas clypeata,* 44

Shrike, Great Grey, *Lanius exc* 394

Shrike, Red-backed, *Lanius col* 392

Silvia cantillans, Subalpine Warb 346

Siskin, *Carduelis spinus,* 428

europaea, Nuthatch, 384

, Arctic, *Stercorarius parasiticus,* 02

, Great, *Stercorarius skua,* 204

ark, *Alauda arvensis,* 282

, *Mergus albellus,* 60

e, *Galinago gallinago,* 184

e, Jack, *Lymnocryptes minimus,* 84

teria mollissima, Eider, 52

ow, House, *Passer domesticus,* 14

ow, Tree, *Passer montanus,* 416

owhawk, *Accipiter nisus,* 128

nbill, *Platalea leucorodia,* 108

ng, *Sturnus vulgaris,* 412

orarius parasiticus, Arctic Skua, 2

orarius skua, Great Skua, 204

a albifrons, Little Tern, 224

a hirundo, Common Tern, 222

a paradisaea, Arctic Tern, 222

a sandvicensis, Sandwich Tern, 0

Black-winged, *Himantopus nantopus,* 156

Little, *Calidris minuta,* 176

chat, *Saxicola torquata,* 320

-curlew, *Burhinus oedicnemus,* 0

White, *Ciconia ciconia,* 106

opelia decaocto, Collared Dove, 6

opelia turtur, Turtle Dove, 238

luco, Tawny Owl, 246

us vulgaris, Starling, 412

ow, *Hirundo rustica,* 288

Bewick's, *Cygnus colombianus,*

Mute, *Cygnus olor,* 12

Swan, Whooper, *Cygnus cygnus,* 14
Swift, *Apus apus,* 256
Swift, Apline, *Apus melba,* 258
Sylvia atricapilla, Blackcap, 354
Sylvia borin, Garden Warbler, 352
Sylvia communis, Whitethroat, 350
Sylvia curruca, Lesser Whitethroat, 348

T
Tachybaptus ruficollis, Little Grebe, 82
Tadorna tadorna, Shelduck, 30
Teal, *Anas crecca,* 36
Tern, Arctic, *Sterna paradisaea,* 222
Tern, Black, *Chidlonias niger,* 224
Tern, Common, *Sterna hirundo,* 222
Tern, Little, *Sterna albifrons,* 224
Tern, Sandwich, *Sterna sandvicensis,* 220
Tetrao tetrix, Black Grouse, 68
Tetrao urogallus, Capercaillie, 70
Thrush, Mistle, *Turdus viscivorus,* 334
Thrush, Song, *Turdus philomelos,* 330
Tit, Bearded, *Panurus biarmicus,* 370
Tit, Blue, *Parus caeruleus,* 380
Tit, Coal, *Parus ater,* 378
Tit, Crested, *Parus cristatus,* 376
Tit, Great, *Parus major,* 382
Tit, Long-tailed, *Aegithalos caudatus,* 372
Tit, Marsh, *Parus palustris,* 374
Tit, Penduline, *Remiz pendulinus,* 370
Tit, Willow, *Parus montanus,* 374
Treecreeper, *Certhia familiaris,* 388
Treecreeper, Short-toed, *Certhia brachydactyla,* 388
Tringa erythropus, Spotted Redshank, 192
Tringa glareola, Wood Sandpiper, 196

Tringa nebularia, Greenshank, 194
Tringa ochropus, Green Sandpiper, 196
Tringa totanus, Redshank, 192
Troglodytes troglodytes, Wren, 306
Turdus iliacus, Redwing, 332
Turdus merula, Blackbird, 326
Turdus philomelos, Song Thrush, 330
Turdus pilaris, Fieldfare, 328
Turdus torquatus, Ring Ouzel, 324
Turdus viscivorus, Mistle Thrush, 334
Turnstone, *Arenaria interpres*, 200
Twite, *Carduelis flavirostris*, 432
Tyto alba, Barn Owl, 242

U
Upupa epops, Hoopoe, 264
Uria aalge, Guillemot, 226

V
Vanellus vanellus, Lapwing, 170
Vulture, Egyptian, *Neophron percnopterus*, 118
Vulture, Griffon, *Gyps fulvus*, 118

W
Wagtail, Grey, *Motacilla cinera*, 298
Wagtail, Pied, *Motacilla alba*, 300
Wagtail, Yellow, *Motacilla flava*, 296
Warbler, Cetti's, *Cettia cetti*, 336
Warbler, Garden, *Sylvia borin*, 352
Warbler, Grasshopper, *Locustella naevia*, 338
Warbler, Icterine, *Hippolais icterina*, 344
Warbler, Melodius, *Hippolais*

polyglotta, 344
Warbler, Reed, *Acrocephalus scirpaceus*, 342
Warbler, Sedge, *Acrocephalus schoenobaenus*, 340
Warbler, Subalpine, *Silvia cantilla* 346
Warbler, Willow, *Phylloscopus trochilus*, 360
Warbler, Wood, *Phylloscopus sibilatrix*, 356
Waxwing, *Bombycilla garrulus*, 3
Wheatear, *Oenanthe oenanthe*, 32
Whimbrel, *Numenius phaeopus*,
Whinchat, *Saxicola rubetra*, 318
Whitethroat, *Sylvia communis*, 3.
Whitethroat, Lesser, *Sylvia curru* 348
Wigeon, *Anas penelope*, 32
Woodcock, *Scolopax rusticola*, 1
Woodlark, *Lullula arborea*, 280
Woodpecker, Black, *Dryocopus martius*, 272
Woodpecker, Great Spotted, *Dendrocopos major*, 274
Woodpecker, Green, *Picus viridis* 270
Woodpecker, Grey-headed, *Picus canus*, 268
Woodpecker, Lesser Spotted, *Dendrocopos minor*, 276
Wren, *Troglodytes troglodytes*, 3
Wryneck, *Jynx torquilla*, 266

Y
Yellowhammer, *Emberiza citrine* 448